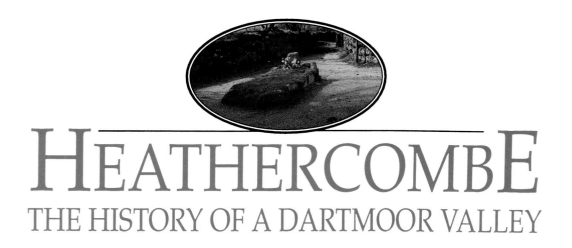

HEATHERCOMBE
THE HISTORY OF A DARTMOOR VALLEY

CLAUDE PIKE

WESTCOUNTRY
— BOOKS —

The longhouse at North Heathercombe.

INTRODUCTION

'albiet the greatest part of this county is of its own nature barren, and full of brakes and briars. Nevertheless, by the industry of man and God's blessing withal, it yieldeth plenty and variety of all things for the use of man . . .'

A Chorographical Survey of Devon Tristram Risdon, 1630.

In the summer of 1991, the Trustees of the Claude and Margaret Pike Woodlands Trust agreed to support me in the preparation of an archaeological and historical survey of the Heathercombe estate, and its environs, for the purpose of recording for posterity man's impact and influence on this secluded part of Dartmoor, from prehistoric times to the present day.

Claude and Margaret Pike at Heathercombe.

In carrying out this project, I have consulted Dr Tom Greeves MA, PhD; Mr. R.J. Pidgeon, RAI.; Mrs. Henrietta Quinnell, BA., FSA.; Mr. Norman Quinnell; Canon J. A. Thurmer, MA., Hon.DD.; J. P. Allen BA., M.Phil; Susan Eward, MA., FSA.; Salisbury librarian, Penelope Walker Boles; Exeter librarian, Tony Vincent, BSc.; Roger Lines; Kevin Bastow; Miss Deborah Hannaford; Robin Stanes and others. I am most grateful for the help and advice I have received.

As my investigation proceeded, more and more topics were discovered to be of interest. These I have described in a certain amount of detail, leaving those particularly interested to investigate them further, indicating some of the sources of further information available. Mistakes may have been made and differing conclusions may be drawn, for which I seek the reader's forbearance.

Inextricably linked with this survey is the overall history of the landscape of Dartmoor within the County of Devon which bears witness to generations of mankind. Through his ceaseless toil man has created the landscape we see around us, the patchwork of wood and field hemmed in by streams and lanes. This volume seeks to explain a little about the influence of the past upon the present, and to provide a record for future generations.

Claude Drew Pike OBE, DL, MA, LL.M, LLD (Hon).
Trustee Claude and Margaret Pike Woodlands Trust

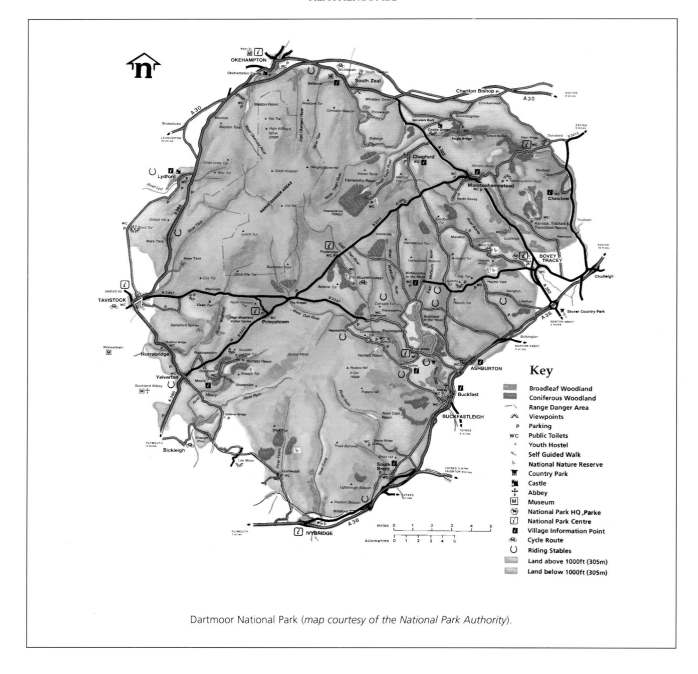

Dartmoor National Park (*map courtesy of the National Park Authority*).

CONTENTS

DEDICATION

To Margaret

TOPOGRAPHY

The Heathercombe estate comprises 237.6 acres (96.2ha) on the eastern edge of the higher moor of Dartmoor, Devon. The land slopes steeply from Hameldown, the highest point of which reaches 1647 ft (532m), to the north-to-south running valley known as Heathercombe. Here three small tributary streams run from the moor to the central watercourse known as the Heathercombe Brook. The valley floor descends to 950 ft (289m) at its lowest point within the estate. To the east a gentler slope rises to the open land of Vogwell and Heatree Downs at between 1148 ft (350m) and 1358 ft (414m) before descending to another north-to-south valley, where lie two outliers of the main estate, upon the east-facing hill slope, approximately 1 mile (1.6km) to the east – Badger Wood. Another separate part of the estate is situated at the head of the second valley at an altitude of 1247 ft (380m) (See Map 2 – Jay's Grave Wood).

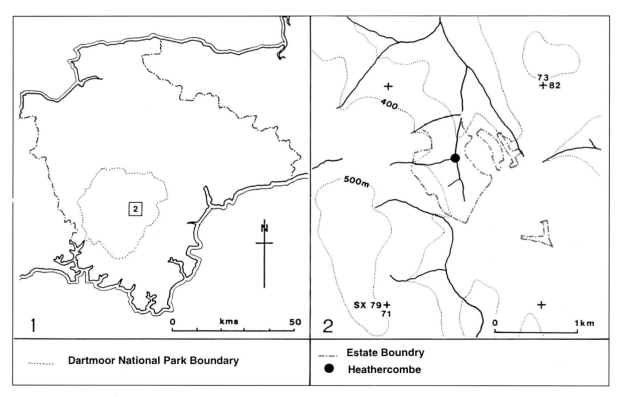

Map 1: Local Map showing the location of Dartmoor within the county of Devon and the Heathercombe estate boundary with the National Park.

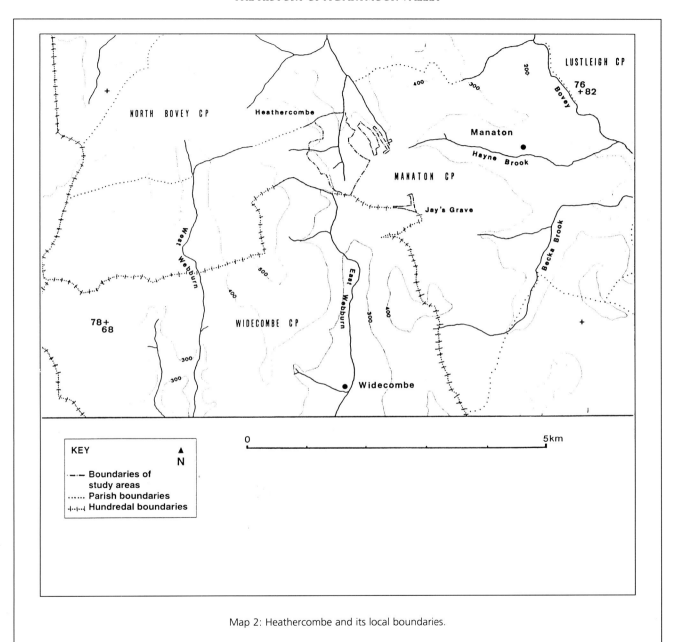

Map 2: Heathercombe and its local boundaries.

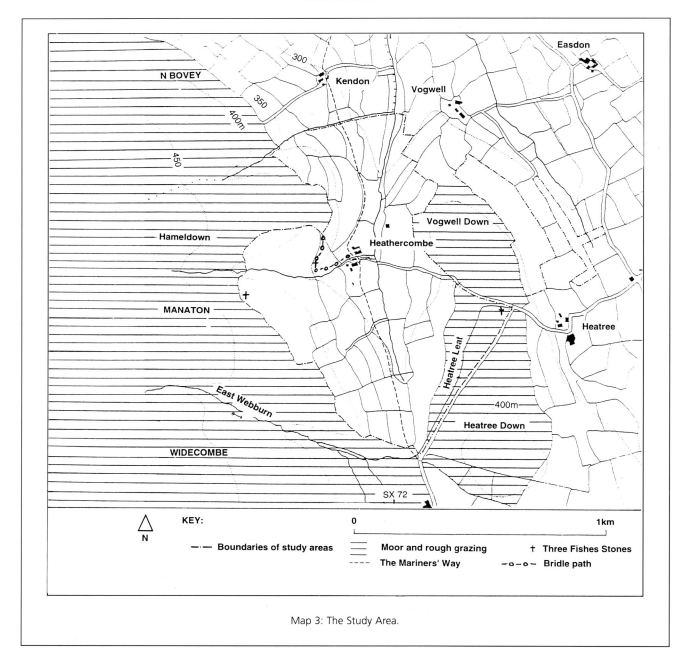

Map 3: The Study Area.

Heathercombe valley from the east with Hameldown rising beyond.

GEOLOGY

'. . . the inhabitants of a civilised country are much governed in their occupation, all other things being equal, by the geological structure of that country . . .'
Henry I. de la Beche, 1839.

The Heathercombe estate is situated on the Dartmoor granite outcrop. These igneous rocks were formed at the end of the Carboniferous period, or the beginning of the Permian Age, as the molten granite was intruded within a varied assemblage of sedimentary rocks. The granite at Heathercombe is coarse grained granite, of the type which forms most of the tors and high level ridges on Dartmoor. It contains large crystals of felspar set in a course matrix of quartz and biotite. Alteration of the granite occurred through the process of mineralisation, including the hydrothermal emplacement of, for example, black tourmaline. The large deposits of tin were the result of these processes.

The present form of Dartmoor was created by various earth movements: one at the end of the Carboniferous period resulted in mountain building and crustal melting over the whole of the South West of England. Another, in the Tertiary period, caused widespread dislocation on north-west/south-east fault lines, notably in the Bovey Tracey, Lustleigh and Sticklepath areas, which were affected by the Sticklepath Fault.

The early rivers eroded the granite and dissected the Dartmoor dome into open valleys. The earliest rivers flowed east. Traces of this drainage pattern are still preserved by the east-west moorland sections of the rivers Dart and Plym. The development of the drainage during the Tertiary period was interrupted by the rising of the sea to 600 ft (183m) above the present O.D.level, isolating Dartmoor as an island.

When the sea retreated, rivers occupied new courses across the emerging sea floor. The ancient course of the Dart eastward, past Ashburton to the mouth of the Teign, was re-occupied until, at a later stage, river capture took place at Holne, diverting the Dart to its present course. (Clayden, 1906;165. Durrance & Laming 1985;129)

The Weathering of the Granite

The moorland surface is dominated by rock outcrops or tors, which frequently overlook wide, shallow basins produced by different types of weathering. One type acting on the vertical joints, divided the granite into blocks; another through the weathering of horizontal joints, opened clefts parallel to the surface of the hillside. These joints controlled the evolution of the granite landscape by guiding the process of weathering and erosion. For example, weathering due to the action of weakly acid groundwater broke down felspar to form clay minerals — resulting in soft granite called 'growan'

Physical weathering, partly caused by Pleistocene frost action, and partly by the elements, also had the effect of shaping the granite landscape. In the Heathercombe valley, we have areas of gently sloping hillside covering course-grained granite resulting from chemical and physical weathering of closely jointed granite. Such rock is exposed in the quarry near the timber bay. We also have outcrops of granite where the joints were further apart. In one place, an outcrop of particularly large rocks can be seen in the 'Valley of the Rocks', rising above the old mill site. There is thus depicted the very long process of erosion of the granite outcrops which has formed the valley as we find it today.

The central area of the Heathercombe valley has a deposit of peaty and gravelly alluvium, whilst deposits of basin peat to the north of this, and in the second valley floor, correspond with deposits of hill peat on the higher western moor.

KEY

▲
N

▤ Peaty Alluvium
▥ Basin Peat

Map 4: Peat deposits in the Heathercombe Valley.

Hound Tor overlooking Heathercombe. The jagged rocks show the typical effects of weathering on Dartmoor granite.

Artefacts from excavations on Heatree Down undertaken by Mrs Minter in 1968: (top right) stone axes; (top left) worked flints, (bottom) pot sherds.

Kent's Cavern, near Torquay, has provided exciting evidence of early man in Devon.

PREHISTORY

'. . . The longer one stays here the more does the spirit of the Moor sink into one's soul; its vastness and also its charm. When you are out upon its bosom you have left all traces of modern England behind you but, on the other hand, you are conscious everywhere of the homes and the work of the prehistoric people.'

(A letter from Dr Watson to Sherlock Holmes. A. Conan Doyle, 1802. *The Hound of the Baskervilles*).

Old Stone Age (Palaeolithic)
c. 450 000 – 8500 BC.

This vast span of time can be divided into many glacial and interglacial periods, the latter sometimes as warm or warmer than today. The ice sheets, however, never came down as far as Devon, which, of course, was part of the continent of Europe. Mammoth, cave bears, woolley rhinoceros and elk were among the exotic species which roamed the countryside at different periods.

The first human beings moved into Britain around 450 000 BC. They were nomadic, lived in caves and rock shelters, and used flint or stone tools, especially handaxes. The best evidence for human occupation in Devon comes from Kent's Cavern, produced by William Pengelly's excavations between 1865 – 80.

During the height of the last glaciation between c. 25 000 and 15 000 BC there may have been a short period during which humans abandoned Britain. After 15 000 BC the climate became warmer, the ice sheets began to retreat, and human occupation was resumed. Around 10 000 BC the temperature dropped a little, reaching a low point c. 8800 BC, after which it started to rise again rapidly. The best evidence for occupation in this late part of the Palaeolithic period comes again from Kent's Cavern, where human bones, in association with reindeer, bison and horse, have been dated by radiocarbon (Smith, 1992;76). The inhabitants of Kent's Cavern dark-haired Iberians may have foraged widely over the terrain between the south-east slopes of Dartmoor and the coast, although no actual material survives from Dartmoor (Todd, 1987;51).

The Middle Stone Age (Mesolithic)
c. 8500 – 4000 BC

As the ice sheets receded, the temperature rose rapidly to reach a 'climatic optimum', somewhat warmer than today, around 6000 BC. The land, which had had a tundra-like vegetation, was gradually colonised by trees, first birch (*Betula nana*), then willow (*Salix alba*), then pine (*Pinus sylvestris*). The few inhabitants, at this time, lived by hunting, fishing from rivers, and gathering from a range of berry-bearing shrubs such as bilberry, blackberry, cranberry and crowberry.

The characteristic artefacts of the Mesolithic period were typically small flint tools known as microliths, often found on sites sheltered in river valleys, for example at Postbridge.

By 6500 BC the warmer climate had melted the ice sheets sufficiently to cause a substantial rise in sea level, resulting in the creation of the English Channel and in Britain becoming an island. The warmer climate caused the development of mixed deciduous forest dominated by oak (*Quercus robur*), with hazel (*corylus*) and elm (*Ulmus procera*) other major components. This would have blanketed Dartmoor up to around 1200 ft (385m).

The New Stone Age (Neolithic)
c. 4000 – 2000 BC

The New Stone Age saw the establishment of the first farming communities in Britain, based on domesticated cattle, sheep, pigs and goats, and on cereals such as emmer, a primitive form of wheat, brought in from the Continent. Improved flint and stone tools, especially axes, enabled these first farmers to start extensive forest clearings. A typical Neolithic axe and an arrowhead were found in the excavations at Heatree Down and many other scatters of Neolithic flint implements have been found on Dartmoor. Houses of this date have not yet been found on Dartmoor, but elsewhere, such as that at Haldon in Devon, they were fairly substantial rectangular structures built of timber. At this time there were highly organised cities in the Euphrates, Tigris and Nile valleys!

The Bronze Age c. 2000—600 BC

The first metal, copper, had been introduced into Britain by people using Beaker pottery in the late Neolithic period. The use of bronze (copper alloyed with about 10% tin) became established around 2000 BC. The knowledge of metals may have been spread by intinerant craftsmen from the Continent.

The climate continued warmer than today through the second millennium BC, with perhaps longer, drier summers than before; average temperatures may have been 2 degrees C above those of today. Clearance of trees and scrub from Dartmoor was very extensive and much open grassland, with some bracken and heather, developed. This millennium saw overall the greatest colonisation of the moor in its history.

Burials in round barrows and cairns, together with the construction of ritual monuments – stone rows and circles – started in the third millennium BC but probably reached their peak soon after 2000 BC in the Early Bronze Age. Dartmoor had contacts with other areas, in particular Wessex. There, elaborate burials are found, often with exotic grave goods, such as faience beads, the product of a craft which originated in the eastern Mediterranean.

One Dartmoor burial, which shows some possible Wessex influence, has been excavated in a cairn known as Two Barrows on Hameldown (Butler, 1991. 148. No 11). This revealed one of the finest specimens of Early Bronze Age craftmanship ever found in Britain – a bronze dagger with a pommel fashioned of amber and decorated with hundreds of tiny gold pins hammered into it (Gill, 1970. 66). This was lost through enemy action in 1942, when Plymouth was bombed.

Our knowledge of prehistoric agriculture will always be handicapped by the acid nature of moorland soil which destroys bone and can badly damage pottery and metals. Information gained from other areas of the country, where animal bones survive and grain, preserved through charring, has been studied, can be applied. The principal domestic animals continued to be cattle, sheep and pigs, all smaller than today. The sheep were hairier and looked much more like goats. Cereals were emmer wheat and barley, both usually spring sown. Celtic beans, rather like a small version of broad beans, were also grown. The proportions of arable to stock varied with local conditions; on Dartmoor it is likely that the emphasis was on stock. People appear to have been skilled at their various crafts and produced clothing of well-woven woollen cloth.

Evidence for Bronze Age occupation on Dartmoor survives in the form of numerous hut circles, pounds or enclosures, and field systems. Many of the latter were laid out in accord with an extensive system of boundaries know as reaves which appear to have been constructed 1600 – 1500 BC around the more habitable lower edge of the Moor (Fleming, 1988).

By the Late Bronze Age the climate deteriorated, and there appears to have been a shift of settlement away from Dartmoor. Centuries of intensive pastural and arable husbandry had largely eliminated the original forest cover, remaining woodland being largely confined to the lowest slopes and valley bottoms. This onset of colder, wetter conditions saw the beginning of the formation of extensive peat deposits, leading to the picture of heathland, with

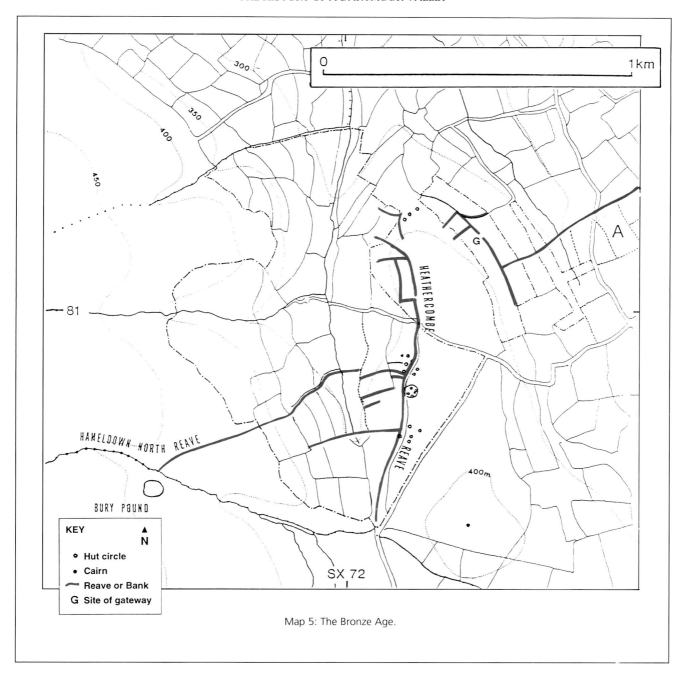

Map 5: The Bronze Age.

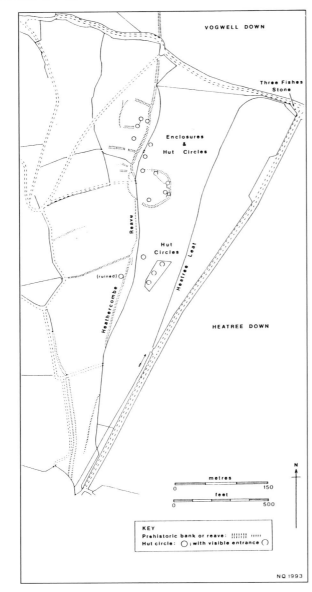

Map 6: Hut circles and enclosures on Heatree Down.

only remnants of oak woodland, which characterizes the Dartmoor we see today.

The Iron Age c. 600 BC to the Roman Conquest

The climate continued cool and wet, and extensive areas of peat continued to grow on the moor. Most of the population moved away, probably living below the 500 ft contour.

Iron tools increased the ability to clear woodland from lower areas still unsettled. Construction of defensive earthworks seems to have begun in Devon by at least the third century BC. Cranbrook Castle, probably never finished, and dating to the first century BC, is an example, perhaps also is Hunter's Tor.

Only occasional Iron Age settlements occur in sheltered positions on Dartmoor. The best known is at Kestor, where iron was actually worked. Small groups may have remained around the moorland edge, but evidence for them is difficult to find. It was during this period that the mostly fair or red haired Celts swarming across northern Europe arrived in England to mix with the dark haired Iberians. They were skilled in ironwork which was then replacing bronze. (Trevellion, 1941; 2–11).

There is no evidence of occupation on Dartmoor in Roman times, or indeed until the later Saxon period after AD 700.

Heathercombe

Evidence for life in the Bronze Age survives on the Heathercombe estate where reaves, fields, huts circles and an enclosure may indicate a larger population and a degree of land management greater even than today's. The archaeological remains indicating this are situated on the drier, more sheltered eastern and south-eastern slopes of the valley, and represent the typical mixed farming lifestyle of the second millennium BC. The hut circles, the remains of substantial circular stone and timber houses, have been found in small groups, some associated with small square fields (Map 5). The Heathercombe reave runs for over a thousand yards (1km) up the east side of the valley. It abuts a pound enclosing at least six hut circles; the enclosure would appear to have been constructed first. But fields had been laid out in places on the downhill side of the reave; the wall of one of these incorporates a typical hut circle. The relationship which the Heathercombe reave has with other monuments are typical of reaves in general and confirms how reaves are closely associated with other Bronze Age sites on the Moor. Hut circles survive on both sides of the reave. It should be remembered that monuments of all types may have been destroyed with the passage of time, particularly because of later land clearance and wall building, and that those which do survive may not present a complete picture of the landscape in prehistory.

Mrs E. M. Minter excavated a group of the hut circles on Heatree Down in the summer of 1968, on behalf of the Devon Archaeological Society (page 18). Unfortunately ill-health and her subsequent death prevented the publication of a report on these excavations. Henrietta Quinnell was commissioned by the Archaeological Society in 1992 to prepare a report for its *Proceedings* (Quinnell No 49, 1991). She had access to Mrs Minter's records but drew her own conclusions on their interpretation. The excavations involved the complete stripping of the interiors of three adjacent, similar, hut circles but no structural features, walls or flooring, were removed. A scatter of artefacts suggested that the site had been occupied intermittently from the Neolithic onward.

The hut circles had stone walls enclosing floors about 20 ft across. All the floors contained traces of post-holes in which substantial timber uprights had been set, and stake-holes where small timbers had been directly driven into the ground. It was not possible to detect a regular internal pattern of posts supporting the roofs; the rafters may have rested directly on the stone walls, with a central post in

Reconstruction of a Bronze Age hut, prior to being 'thatched'. *(Courtesy Mr Lawrence)*.

some cases. Most of the timberwork would have related to internal divisions and furnishings. There was only one definite internal hearth – it is possible that these hut circles represented seasonal occupation, sleeping places used in summer. After a period of abandonment all three circles were repaired, with more stone used in their floors and less evidence of timber fitments.

Finds were scarce, and there was no material suitable for radiocarbon dating. Pottery sherds suggested a date in the later second millennium BC, a date possibly to be extended to the tenth or ninth centuries. Thereafter the circles were abandoned, following the general movement of population away from the moor at this stage.

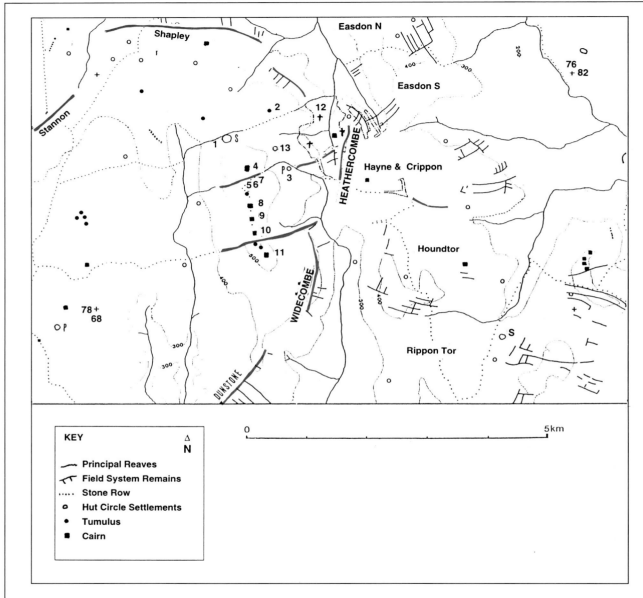

Easdon N

Shapley

Easdon S

76
+ 82

Stannon

2

12
+

13

P
3

4

5 6 7

8

9

10

11

HEATHERCOMBE

Hayne & Crippon

Houndtor

WIDECOMBE

78 +
68

O P

Rippon Tor

S

DUNSTONE

KEY

△
N

⌢ Principal Reaves
⊤⊤ Field System Remains
..... Stone Row
o Hut Circle Settlements
• Tumulus
▪ Cairn

0   5km

Map 7: Prehistoric and modern sites and monuments in the Heathercombe Valley.

HAMELDOWN CAIRNS AND MONUMENTS (See Map 7)

1. **Grimspound** – This consists of twenty-four hut circles surrounded by a double-faced wall.

2. **King's Barrow** – on the summit of King Tor. Recorded in 1872 to have been excavated without result.

3. **Berry Pound** – possibly contemporary with Grimspound.

4. **Hameldown Tor** – Surmounted by a low cairn (on which an Ordnance Survey triangulation pillar has been erected).

5. **Hameldown Cross** – A medieval cross utilized as a boundstone and inscribed 'HC DS 1854'.

6. **Grey Wethers** – A boundary stone. The name is occasionally applied to a stone which, from a distance, may resemble a sheep.

7. **Blue Jug** – A boundary stone.

8. **Broad Barrow** – One of the largest barrows on Dartmoor; it contains one of the Dukestones—DS 1854.

9. **Single Barrow** – Crowned by a Dukestone of 1854. Barrow excavated 1873, when a Bronze Age cremation was found.

10. **Two Barrows** – A pair of burial mounds excavated in 1872, in one of which was a cremation accompanied by a Bronze Age dagger with amber pommel inlaid with gold pins, dated about 1500 BC. Destroyed when Plymouth Museum was bombed in 1941.

11. **Hameldown Beacon** – A prehistoric cairn surmounted by a Dukestone. Also site of one of a chain of beacons which once relayed signals across the interior of the county.

12. **Three Fishes Stones** – These three stones were erected by Claude Pike between 1969 and 1977. (See under section 'Heathercombe Crosses—Doxology to The Lord's Prayer').

13. **Hameldown Memorial Stone** – This stone commemorates a tragic event in 1941, when five British airmen lost their lives, their plane having crashed in a mist which enshrouded Hameldown. The date and the airmen's initials are engraved upon a massive 6ft high stone, which was erected by Mr Alec Kitson of Heatree House and Mr Charlie Hannaford of Natsworthy. Looks like a sheep at a distance.

REFERENCES

Fox A. 1957 *Archaeological Journal* 114; 15B.

Bate C.S. 1872, *Trans. Devon Assn.* 5; 549–567.

Grinsell L.V. 1978, 'Dartmoor Barrows'. *Proc. Devon. Arch. Soc.* 36; 154.

Phillips E.M. 1937. *Trans. Devon Assn.* 69; 330.

Grinsell (as above) p.155.

Rowe S. 1848 (1985 Edn.) 148 (and Grinsell, as above, p.155).

Rowe S. 1848 (1986 Edn.) 147 (and Grinsell, as above, p.156).

Grinsell (as 4) p. 176. Butler J. 1991—*Dartmoor Atlas of Antiquities* 1; 148.

THE ROMAN PERIOD

After the Roman Invasion in AD 43, a Roman legion eventually entered Devon in about AD 50–55, in the reign of Nero (AD 54 – 65.). The Celtic inhabitants of Devon at that time were the Dumnonii. A legionary fortress was built in Exeter, the troops spreading out beyond to Topsham, Okehampton, North Tawton and Tiverton, all to the north of Dartmoor. Beyond Exeter the Romanisation of the population appears to be only superficial.

The Iron Age farming settlements, and the Celtic kingdom of the Dumnonii, continued almost unaffected (Costen 1992; 34).

Some signs of Christianity appeared before the middle of the fourth century as the influence and power of the Roman Empire declined towards the end of that century. Exeter began showing signs of decay and by the early fifth century, urban life in the Roman sense had ceased, long before the arrival of the Saxons.

THE DARK AGES

About two-and-a-half centuries lapsed between the end of the Roman rule and the arrival of the Saxons in Devon. In this period the native Celtic population was thinned out by plague, particularly by the yellow plague (probably a form of hepatitis) in AD 540, and by migration to Brittany, partly because of the breakdown in law and order (Mildren, 1988; 17).

This left the Celts in no position to resist the Saxons in 577 at the battle of Dyrham, north of Bath, and later, when the Saxons invaded Devon in the seventh century. Little of the written historical record remains of the period AD 450 to 600, known as the Age of the Saints, during which the Christian faith flourished among the Celts long before St Augustine came to convert the heathen English.

THE COMING OF THE SAXONS

The Saxons entered the South West in the early seventh century, at which time the population was ill-placed to resist. The leading role in the invasion was played by the kings of Wessex.

The Battle of Peonnun, in AD 658, was fought, it is thought, just east of Exeter, the frontier of Selwood forest having been broken (Costen 1992;81) and that of Posentesburh in AD 661, perhaps at Posbury, a commanding hill fort a little north-east of Dartmoor. In AD 682, King Centwin pushed the Britons to the Atlantic coast of north-east Cornwall, with all Devon north of Dartmoor falling into Saxon hands. In AD 710, Ine, King of the West Saxons, defeated Geraint, King of the Dumnonii, and completed the conquest of Devon, but the Celtic populace survived (Gibbs, 1981;15).

The north-east side of the moor was colonised as far south as about Manaton. The Saxons did not settle on open moorland above the 1000 ft (320m) contour. It was the land at the height of between 500 and 1000 ft which attracted them. They were great axemen, and began in earnest clearing the valleys and carving farms out of forests (of oak, ash and beech) and waste, helped by a change to a comparatively warm and dry climate. The lower lands and deep valleys had been heavily wooded, and had been quite beyond the earlier primitive means of clearance. By the ninth century, the higher ground had become a hunting ground for the Wessex kings.

Farms began to be established on what is today called open moorland. Cultivation began with ploughing contourwise along the slopes. The shape of many fields being used today in the Widecombe valley, and elsewhere, suggests such an origin. The most obvious strip cultivation is found in the valley of the upper West Webburn in Widecombe and Manaton parishes, and particularly on the east side of Challacombe Down. The villagers of Challacombe

Lynchets on the hillside at Challacombe.

cultivated strips (called lynchets) on the steep hillside over a long period of time. On the Hameldown side of the valley similar, but much smaller, layouts can be seen (*Dartmoor from the Air* Greeves, 1985;14).

In the ninth and tenth centuries, the Saxons had to contend with the invasions by the Vikings from Denmark (Hoskins, 1953; 52–53). In the late ninth century, King Alfred (848, r. 871–899) after his victory in AD 878, constructed a number of fortified sites to counter these invasions (Costen, 1992; 113). These attacks, nevertheless, continued.

In AD 997, the Danes pillaged and burnt the Benedictine Tavistock Abbey and sacked Kingsteignton in 1001 (Athelred 'The Unready' 966 r. 979–1006). It may be that farms on the higher grounds of Dartmoor, as recorded in Domesday Survey, were not seriously affected by the invasions of the Danes and Vikings in the two centuries before the Norman Conquest.

By the early eleventh century, colonisation of the higher ground above 1000 ft (320m) had taken place (King Canute 995, r. 1017–1035).

It has been discovered that beneath the ruins of

The 'longhouse' Houndtor medieval village.

stonewalled houses, which first attracted attention, are signs of the post holes of earlier wattle and turf huts – built and then rebuilt on almost identical sites on several occasions. The best known example is the Hound Tor medieval village, where up to ten buildings have been noted. The settlements were hamlets of several buildings – eleven at Hound Tor, thirteen at Blackaton, and twelve at Challacombe.

These settlements were perhaps of the eleventh and twelfth centuries, rather than earlier, as suggested by Mrs Minter.

In the four centuries between the arrival of the Saxons and the Norman Conquest, nearly all the present villages, and most of the hamlets, had been founded. The foundation of Devon, as district from Celtic Dumnonii, had been solidly laid.

THE NORMAN INVASION 1066

On the death of Edward the Confessor in AD 1066, Duke William of Normandy invaded England, defeated Harold and became king. To the vast majority of the people on the farms on and around Dartmoor, the Norman invasion initially made little or no practical difference (Costen, 1992; 166) unlike the Saxon invasion which, it is claimed, was followed by wholesale displacement of many of the early Britons (but see Gibbs, 1981; 15).

The landlords, however, were displaced and their lands given to the new Norman landlords (Stenton, 1990; 626). Even small landowners suffered (Costen, 1992; 165). For example, Baldwin was made Sheriff of Devon and given large areas of land in the County (Costen, 1992; 152: Stenton, 1990; 632).

The manorial system was quite well established by the year AD 1066, but soon after the Norman invasion the Normans expanded this into the feudal system, every man being subject to his overlord. The landholding, as a pyramid, rose up tier on tier to the king until every acre in the country was held of somebody by some form of service, varying from knight's service to the king at the top of the pyramid, to service of the lord of the manor by the villagers, at the bottom.

The Normans created Dartmoor as a royal forest, where the beasts of the forest – deer, hare, boar and wolf– were strictly preserved, with harsh penalties for transgressing the law.

The Domesday Survey AD 1086

The Anglo-Saxon Chronicle records that in 1085, King William I (1025, r.1066 – 1087) sent men all over England – to each shire – to find out what, and how much, each landlord held in land and livestock, and what it was worth. A second set of commissioners was sent, without warning, to check the returns. These returns were collected at Winchester and collated into a volume known as the Domesday Book.

Apart from the king wanting to know what he had, the commissioners listed lands in dispute arising out of the seizure of land by the Norman-invading barons. In due course it became the final authorative register of rightful possession. It was, in consequence, called the Domesday Book by an analogy from The Day of Judgement. It described the old English society under new management, foreign lords having taken over.

It was written in Latin on the skins of about 190 sheep by a single scribe.

The lands in Devon were entered in Hundreds. The attached schedule indicates the kind of information contained in the survey, as far as the land in the vicinity of Heathercombe is concerned.

Dartmoor as such is not mentioned by name. The survey refers to both pastoral and other land in the various manors. The manors lying below Hameldown seem to have pastures much smaller in extent than one would have expected. The pattern of farmsteads thinly scattered over the whole area was one which varied only slightly over the next two centuries. The great majority of farms had already been founded, and the ensuing years were years of consolidation rather than fresh settlements.

The Exeter Domesday

For the south-western counties there exists the Exon Domesday Book, which appears to be a preliminary draft for the great Domesday Book. This is now kept in the Exeter Diocesan Library.

Slavery

It will be seen from the Domesday Summary of the Teignbridge Hundred that a substantial number of slaves are recorded. Slavery had obviously existed for a considerable time, but little is written as to the law governing slavery, unlike the comprehensive Body of Law dealing with slavery in the Roman Empire.

DOMESDAY SURVEY – 1086

	Teignbridge Hundred						Haytor Hundred
	Manors						
	Bovey Tracey	Bagtor	North Bovey	Manaton		Shapley	Natsworthy
				Edwin	Aldred		
Landholding	2h	1v	1h 3v	1v	1v	½ h	1f
Land for plough	10	5	8	1	2	3	2
Lordship land	½ h	1f	3v	½ v		1v	
Lordship ploughs	3	1	1	1			
Villagers land	1½ h		1h	½ v		1v	
Villagers ploughs	10	4		1			
Villagers	16	6	11	3	3		2
Smallholders	8	2	6	3	2		2
Slaves	8	1	5	1	1		1
Cattle	30	5	8	10	3	10	
Pigs	7	3	3				
Sheep	85	35	56	30	10	30	
Goats	5	15	15	25		25	
Woodlands	60a	3a	10a	½ lea. +½ furlong	5a		6a
Meadows	5a		20a	5a	1a	5a	5a
Pasture	50a	1 lea. +½ lea.	1 lea	2a 10a			
	£10	20s.	40s.	10s.	20s.	7s.6d.	Natsworthy 15s.*

*Purchased by Duke of Somerset 1854. He had his initial 'D.S.' on the boundary stones (Butler, 1991;151).

v	–	virgate	= 30 acres
h	–	hide	= 120 acres (Costen 1971)
f	–	furlong	= ¼ of virgate – 7½ acres
		league	= 1½ miles

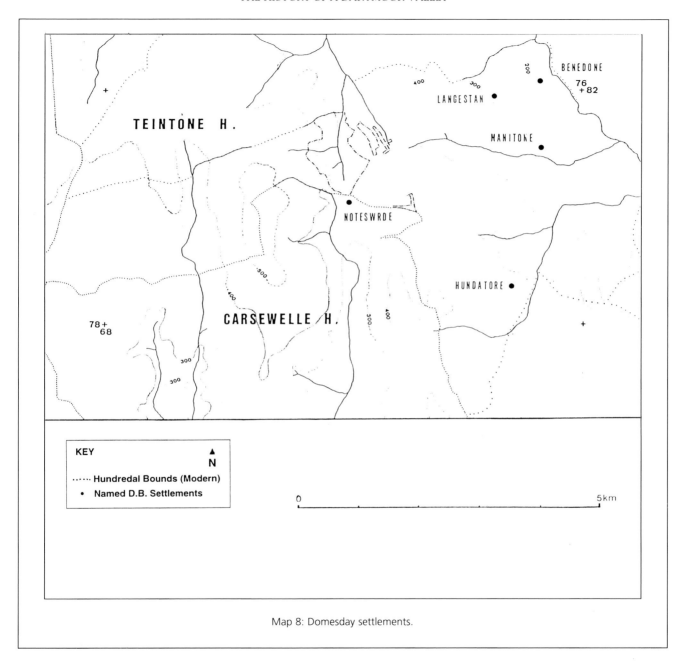

Map 8: Domesday settlements.

It is speculated that slavery probably originated as a result of the Saxon invasion, for it is highly unlikely that the slaves were survivors of the Roman occupation. Trevellion (1937; 147) records that the slave population at the time of Domesday was 9 per cent of the recorded population, and (at p. 66) 'that if a slave worked on Sunday by his lord's command, he should become free'. If, however, a freeman 'works on that day, except by his lord's command, he shall be reduced to slavery'. This law, and others, showed that the church had not set its face against slavery 'at that time'.

Slaves were obviously, from time to time, emancipated, probably at the discretion of their owners (Finberg, 1969; 44).

MEDIEVAL DEVON

The Wool Trade

Wool plays a great part in Devon's historic economy – an industry largely contemporary with the tin trade (Gill, 1970; 120).

The beginnings owed much to the Cistercians of Buckfast Abbey in the twelfth century, and the Benedictines of Tavistock Abbey, which had been founded in AD 974.

We have no detailed knowledge of how Heathercombe valley was inhabited in medieval Devon. Sheep farming with common grazing rights on Hameldown, no doubt, was the main activity of the North and South Heathercombe farms. Moretonhampstead had a fulling mill before the end of the thirteenth century. Chagford was on the old packhorse route for the industry, from North Devon to Ashburton. The route must have passed by Heathercombe.

Devon wool, however, was of low grade, and it is now realised that its importance in the Middle Ages has been overstated. It did, however, benefit from the expansion of the clothing industry in the fifteenth century.

Wealth derived from sheep farming and tin streaming in the valley must have enabled the North and South Heathercombe farmers to lay the foundation of the two longhouses in the valley. It is interesting to note that the Burial in Wool Acts of 1667 and 1668 intended to support the wool trade, enacted that corpses should be buried in woollen shrouds.

Tin Mining in Devon and the Stannary Laws

Little is known of tin mining in Devon in pre-Roman and Roman periods. It was not until after the Dark Ages that the recorded resumption of tin mining took place in the eleventh century.

But Middicott (1989; 43) suggests that King Alfred's wealth could, in part, have been based on revenues from tin mining (King Alfred 848, r. 871–899).

There was no special tin mining law, although certain customs had developed; for example, the custom of bounding tin stream works. This was contrary to the general presumption that the surface owner had title to the minerals. In Devon and Cornwall, there had developed a form of tin bounds and tin bounders' rights.

The transition to medieval mining laws arose out of the provision of a tin toll to the owner of the land, and the payment of coinage duty to the Crown. The earliest records show that tin coinage – the duty – was collected in the late twelfth century, usually by the Sheriff.

It was in 1198 that the Chief Justiciar and Chief Minister of Richard I (Coeur de Lion 1157, r. 1189–1199) issued a writ convening juries of miners to declare the law and practice relating to the coinage. It was from these sessions of twelve jurymen that the Convocations, in Devon known as 'Great Courts', originated.

By 1197, the first Chief Warden of the Stannaries had been appointed, and the writ of 1198 confirmed the 'just and ancient customs and liberties of miners, smelters and merchants of tin', and inhibited the sale of uncoined tin and the transportation of any tin outside Devon without the licence of the Chief Warden, Three years later, King John (1166, r.1199 – 1216) granted free status to the tin miners in Devon, and made them subject only to the jurisdiction of the Chief Warden. The reason given for this emancipation was that the working of tin benefited the king by way of coinage duty.

During the course of the thirteenth century, the courts of the Chief Warden's Stewards, with jurisdiction over the tin miners and tin affairs, were established in the mining districts of Devon and Cornwall. Each district was known as a stannary, the jurisdiction of the Steward being confined to it. The four Stannaries of Devon were centred in Chagford, Ashburton, Tavistock and Plympton; Heathercombe came under the Chagford Stannary.

The Tinners' Charter of Edward I (1239, r. 1271– 1307) in 1305, defined the privileges of the miners. These Charters were confirmed by succeeding monarchs. Working miners, in consequence, could not be brought before the ordinary courts, except upon charges of serious crime, murder, manslaughter, etc., or concerning title to the land. In all other suits, whether relating to tin mining or not, tinners were to be sued, and sue in their Stannary Court. The Charters also exempted tinners from certain royal, feudal and local taxes, market and road tolls, and charges for the use of a particular place in the market town for the sale of goods.

The Tinners Charter of 1305 also authorised tinners to mine for tin and dig turves for smelting tin everywhere in the King's land, moors and wastes, and in those of other persons, provided they had bounded the land in the customary way. Bounding consisted of marking four corner bounds by cutting up turf in each corner, thus marking out the bound. The corners were in due course marked with stones.

The Charter of 1305 directed that all tin should be coined once a year, Tavistock, Ashburton and Chagford being Devon coinage towns (Plympton was added in 1328).

Between the sixteenth and eighteenth centuries, the jurisdiction of the Stannary Courts was substantially expanded, aided by the fact that the administration of the law was almost wholly in the hands of the tinners, for the Vice-Warden and the Stannary Stewards of the Stannary Courts were appointed from among their own ranks.

The Stannary Courts, through the Vice-Warden, endeavoured to secure a wider jurisdiction. In this they succeeded through the Vice-Warden's Courts evolving an equity jurisdiction, as opposed to the Common Law jurisdiction of the Steward's Courts. The Steward's Courts thus in due course became obsolete and were abolished by Act of Parliament in 1836.

The Stannary institutions continued without much change until the first quarter of the nineteenth century; but then disputes arose between the Vice-Warden's Courts and the Court of Common Law. Disputes continued throughout the century, culminating in the Stannaries Court (Abolition) Act of 1896, the Warden's Court ceasing to exist on 1 January, 1897.

Tin Streaming at Heathercombe

In 1991, Dr Tom Greeves, MA, PhD, recorded the development of tin working at Heathercombe. Dr Greeves has indicated that tinners are first documented as being on Dartmoor in the twelfth century, and that from this time onwards there is a continuous historical record until 1930, when the last working mine closed at Golden Dagger on the extreme western edge of Manaton parish.

The industry was very productive in the late twelfth century, but the best documented peak in Devon was during the period 1450 to 1600, Chagford stannary being the leading producer in Devon in the mid fifteenth century. These figures imply that for Heathercombe and Manaton the most widespread activity may well have been before 1500. There is, however, very little documentary evidence of tin working at Heathercombe.

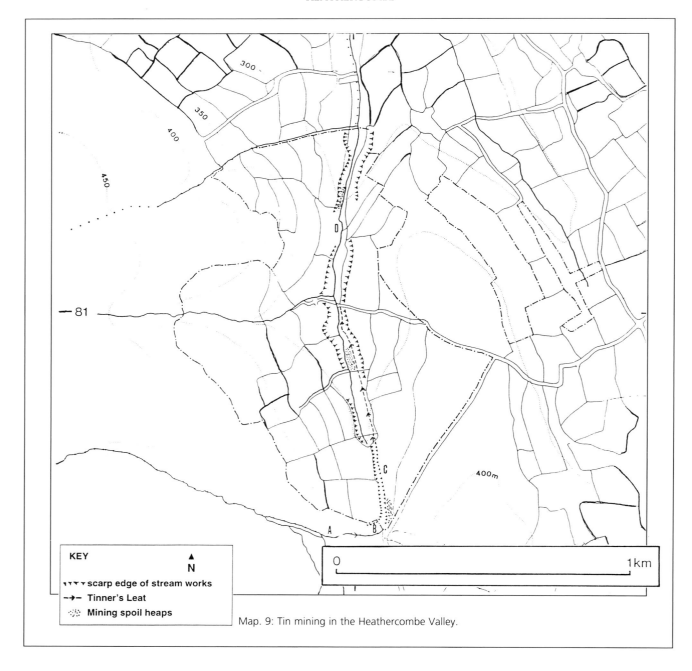

KEY

▲
N

ⱴⱴⱴⱴⱴ scarp edge of stream works

⇢ Tinner's Leat

⋰⋱ Mining spoil heaps

Map. 9: Tin mining in the Heathercombe Valley.

Tin streaming clearly took place at Heathercombe along the bottom of the valley, down from Natsworthy, washed by a leat A–B taken off the East Webburn (as shown on Map 9).

It is interesting to note that the leat from the Webburn is along the Manaton parish boundary. The most likely explanation is that when maps were first drawn, indicating parish boundaries, the leat was an easily identifiable landmark. This leat still exists, having in more recent times, been extended by John Kitson, to supply water to Heatree House and farm, where there is a small reservoir which also supplied water to a water wheel.

One of the many streams running into the valley.

Dr Greeves believes that the Heathercombe Mill, recorded in the tithe apportionment of 1842, as 'ruins of Mill', although theoretically in a good position to serve the tin works, is likely only to have been a corn mill of the early nineteenth century.

There may have been recent connections with the tin working at Heathercombe through the Pethybridge family, who are known to have occupied Heathercombe in the mid nineteenth century. There were several people called Pethybridge involved in tin working Chagford Stannary at an earlier date. For example, William Pethebrygge was a jurate for Chagford Stannary at the Crockerntor Great Court in 1494, and John Pethebrygge was presenting small amounts of tin metal for coinage at Chagford in 1550. (Map 10 shows the location of tin works and mills in and around Heathercombe).

The names of several tin miners active within the Manaton area in the fifteenth and sixteenth centuries are known. These may well have streamed tin at Heathercombe. Heathercombe tin would probably have gone to the knocking mill at Gratnar, or south to Pitton and, for smelting, to the blowing mill at Blackaller at North Bovey; but whichever mill it went to it eventually had to go to Chagford in ingot form. The metal would be sold on the open market after assay and payment of tax.

The name Nosworthy was also known at that time. In 1599, Thomas Nosworthy, the Elder of Manaton, owned a cottage near a blowing mill at Lustleigh. It was from the Nosworthy family that the Kitsons bought the Jay's Grave property in 1893.

It is not known by what right tin mining took place at Heathercombe, whether worked by virtue of a lease granted by the landowner, or by virtue of the tinners having marked out the area for streaming, by right of the custom of tin bounding. The tin streaming taking place at the bottom of the Heathercombe valley would not have materially adversely affected the medieval farming of the time, but one wonders whether or not the cornmill was in operation, during or after the tin streaming. To

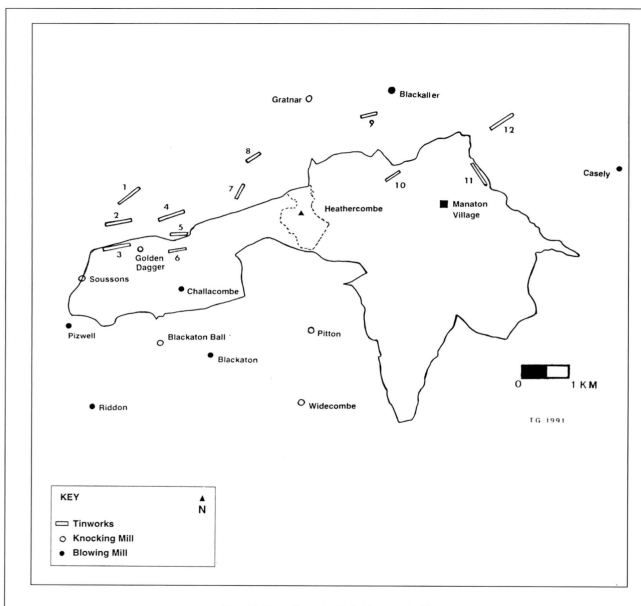

Map 10: Tinworks and mills in Manaton Parish.

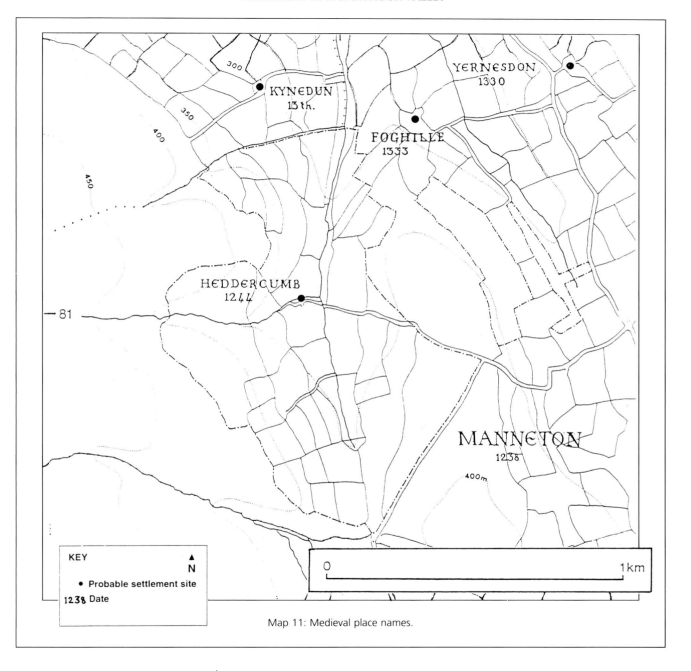

justify a mill there must have been a substantial amount of corn to grind.

Medieval Place-names (see Map 11)

KYNEDUN (Kendon) thirteenth century
  from O.E. 'cyning (cyne) dun' – king or
  royal hill

YERNESDON (Easdon) 1330
  O.E. 'earnes-dun' – eagles hill
  1805 Ordnance Survey – East Devon

HEDDERCUMB (Heathercombe) 1244

HEDERCOMB 1330
  O.E. 'Haedra-cumb' – Hawthorn/heath valley

HATHERCOMBE 1413
  N.B. Not Heather; this plant name was not
  used in southern Britain before modern times.

FOGHILLE (Vogwell) 1333
  M.E. Foggy hill-pasture

MANNETON (Manaton) 1238
  O.B. (ge) 'maene-dun' common (as in
  common land) hill

From Salisbury Cathedral Archives:
  (1274– 1283)

WYDECUMB (Widecombe-in-the-Moor)

CHALVECUMB (Challacombe)

SONESTON (Soussons)

NORTHBOVI (North Bovey)

JOHN MANWOOD'S TREATY OF THE LAW OF THE FOREST – 1598

John Manwood, in the preface to his *Law of the Forest* (first published in 1598), in the 1615 edition said that 'kings and princes were often wearied by the great and weighty affairs of the Common Weale laws had given them royal perogatives and princely pleasures to re-create themselves, and to put away from themselves remembrance of their labour and toil'. Among these perogatives was that of the liberty of the forest.

A forest had for long been a franchise for princely pleasures, to the exclusion of their subjects. Kings, in consequence, had from time to time, afforested areas of land, thus creating places reserved for their pleasure and recreation. As a result, there had developed particular laws of the forest, differing from the Common Law of the Realm.

Those subjects who trespassed in any way in these forests were punished with 'very sharp laws', but the laws were uncertain and the offenders were punished at the king's will, and not by any certain law. But when King Canute came to the throne (994. r.1011–1035) he established certain laws. These John Manwood has placed on record. He also has shown how the laws have been altered and changed from time to time.

Before this time, all wild beasts and birds belonged to the king. King Canute decreed that henceforth a subject can take the 'vert and venison or hunting that he can get upon his own land outside the royal forest'. King Edward the Confessor (r.1047 – 1066) confirmed this law, as did William the Conqueror, William Rufus and Henry I (rs.1066 – 1135) when the areas of forest were specified. King Stephen (r.1125 – 1154) also confirmed the laws, as did Henry II (r.1154 – 1189) in his General Charter. The king could make a forest in any place he pleased, even on the lands of his subjects, which was a great loss to these landowners. After lands had been afforested, the pastures and profits of the lands could be devoured by the beasts of the king without any recompense. As the afforesting of the land continued to increase, it became an extreme burden, both to the rich and the poor owners of the land, for they could no longer improve their land so afforested, failure to comply with the forest laws being severely punished (Crossing *Lydford Law* p.24). This continued under Richard I (r.1189 – 1199) and John (r.1199 – 1216). These kings increased and made more new forests on the lands of their subjects, to their great loss.

Kings Richard, John, and Henry II afforested so much of the lands of their subjects that the greatest part of the realm had become forest. This continued until Henry III (r.1216 – 1272) granted the Charter of the Forests in 1217 to pacify his subjects. By this Charter, all forests that he had imposed on the land belonging to his subjects were disafforested, and all lands afforested by King Richard and King John on the lands of their subjects, were also disafforested (James, 1981; 9).

Since that time, Manwood has recorded that the forest laws had been moderated, so that by 1598, when he wrote his treaties, the laws were very mild. Queen Elizabeth I (r.1533 – 1605) showed clemency in their execution.

Both Elizabeth and James I alienated portions of the royal forests by letting them on lease. Charles I, however, endeavoured to reclaim forests and to revive many of the forest laws which had fallen into disuse, anxious to obtain funds by any means by utilising forest courts to extort fines. It was largely owing to his arbitrary behaviour that in 1640, the Act for the Limitation of Forests was passed, which virtually cancelled the application of forest laws, and forever took away the royal power of afforesting new country (Rogers, 1942; 27). (For more details see N.D.G. James *A History of English Forestry*, 1981).

THE FOREST OF DARTMOOR

The increased afforestation of land by the kings of England after the Norman Conquest appears to have resulted in the whole of Devon being designated a forest.

The increase in population from the twelfth century onwards encouraged encroachment upon the untilled land of the forest. In 1184 – 5, one Richard Fortescue of South Devon was fined one mark for 'waste of forest', i.e. enclosing closed woodland for his own use. The conflict was so great that in 1204, the men of Devon paid King John 5000 marks – a considerable sum – to have the whole of the county, except the forests of Dartmoor and Exmoor, disafforested. A few years later, in 1217, as will have been seen from the Manwood Preface, Henry III (1206, r. 1216 – 1272) signed the Forest Charter disafforesting certain lands not owned by the king, and confirming certain rights and remedies against grievances consequent upon the previously onerous forest laws.

In 1239, Dartmoor forest was granted to Richard Earl of Cornwall, and as a result it ceased to be a forest and became, in law, a chase (which meant the common law applied). On the death of the Earl of Cornwall (1209 – 72) the forest reverted to the Crown and to Henry III's successor, Edward I, who reigned 1272 – 1307.

The forest remained Crown property until the reign of Edward III (r.1327 – 1377)). On 17 March 1337 he made a grant of the forest to his son, Edward, The Black Prince, who then became Prince of the Manor of Lydford and the Chase of Dartmoor; it is still known, however, as the Forest of Dartmoor. Since that time, the forest – the Parish of Lydford – has remained part of the Duchy of Cornwall.

The relaxation of the forest laws by Henry III resulted in the recolonisation of Dartmoor, including the establishment of the 'Ancient Tenements' such as Riddon, Babeny and Pizwel. It was from this time

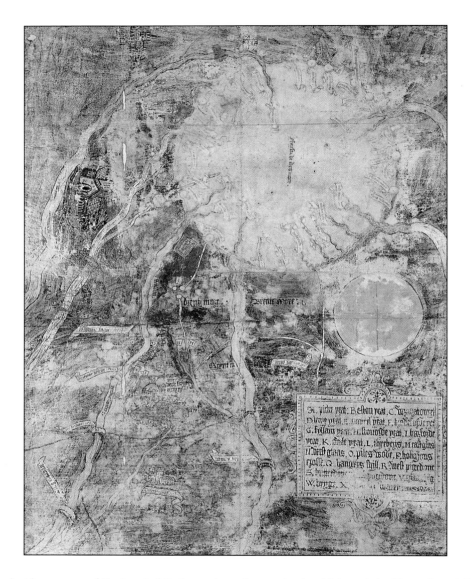

The earliest known map of the Forest of Dartmoor shows the moorland parish boundaries (Devon Record Office).

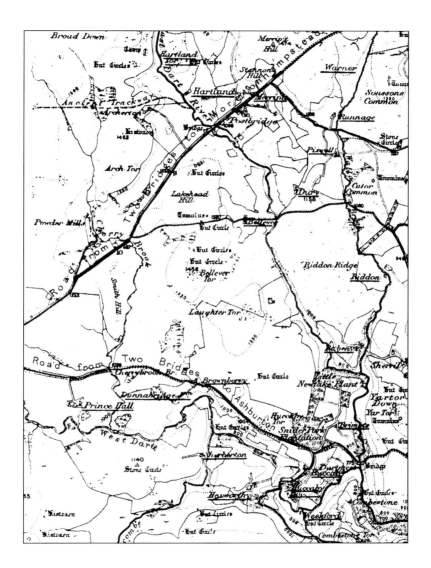

The Ancient Tenements of Dartmoor (from Burnard's *Dartmoor Pictorial Records*).

onwards, from the thirteenth to the seventeenth century, that the piecemeal field enclosures of land of the Commons of Devon, which surrounded the forest, took place. (For a definition of the Forest of Dartmoor and the Commons of Devon see Commons Registration Act 1965, Decision of A. A. Baden Fuller, Commons Commissioner, p.8 – 36, and Gill 1970 p. 153 and Rowe 1985; map 1).

Dartmoor was, in fact, never used a great deal as a hunting ground, owing partly to its distance from London, and partly from the nature of the country – its bogs, rocks and thick mists. The presence of a great number of sheep on Dartmoor at an early date shows how little it was used as a hunting ground, for sheep were strictly excluded from most forests, the smell being much disliked by the deer (Rogers, 1942; 73).

Towards the end of the eighteenth century, the red deer had become so plentiful on Dartmoor that farmers complained, and at last they were exterminated by the Duke of Bedford's stag hounds especially sent down from Woburn. Some red deer, in recent times have found their way down from Exmoor, but the numbers are not as yet numerous.

THE EARLY ENCLOSURES

In Devon, from at least the twelfth century, the pressure of population began to encourage encroachment upon the previously untilled land (Gill, 1970; 154).

At Heathercombe, the enclosing of land is apparent across most of the estate, but particularly towards the western open moor, where large irregular fields clinging to the valley side, show secondary subdivisions from the original single enclosures denoted by one single name, usually prefixed by the nature of the subdivision. Examples of these are as follows (refer to the 1842 Tithe Map and Apportionment Schedule for field names and numbers):

Nos. 88, 89, 90, 91	Higher, Middle, Lower and Broad Park Brake
Nos. 92, 94	Higher and Lower Moor
Nos. 376, 377	Stainty Park
Nos. 391, 391	Homer and Yonder Eastern Close
Nos. 394, 395	Lower and Higher Long Place
Nos. 397, 398	Higher and Lower Hewstone Park
Nos. 399, 400	Higher and Lower Hewstone Park ('Park' meaning enclosed land)

On the eastern side of the valley the development is more obscured where historic boundaries have not provided such a clear enclosure pattern to be seen or recorded, although the area covered by the fields 387, 388, 389 and 390 seem to follow a similar pattern. From the overall picture it seems that through the medieval period through to the nineteenth century, at least, North and South Heathercombe developed as separate entities (see Tithe Map and Apportionment 1842). Greater development occurred to the south of the valley, compared to the north, where parish bounds and difficult terrain restricted growth.

Newtakes continued until 1780, when the tenant's right to make newtakes was abolished. The large Heathercombe Newtake to the west of the valley was no doubt enclosed in the eighteenth century.

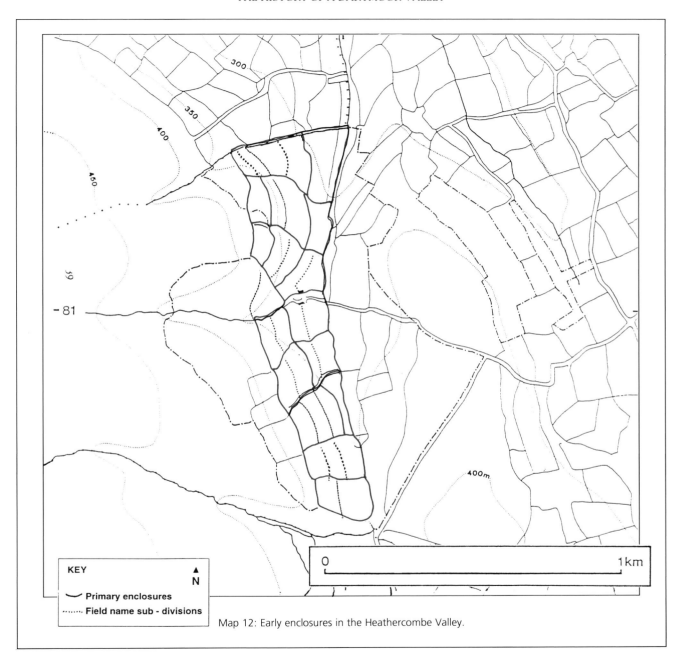

KEY

⌣ **Primary enclosures**

········ **Field name sub - divisions**

▲
N

Map 12: Early enclosures in the Heathercombe Valley.

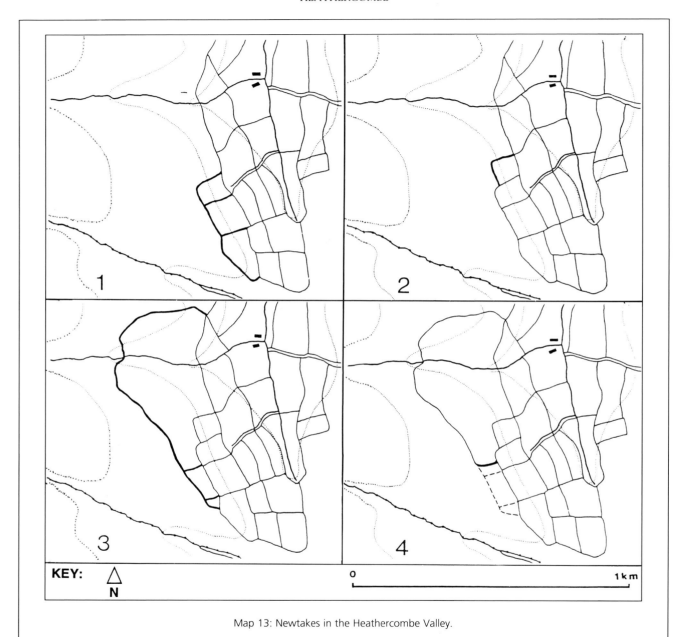

KEY: N

0   1km

Map 13: Newtakes in the Heathercombe Valley.

THE
LONGHOUSES[†]

NORTH AND SOUTH HEATHERCOMBE

". . . I found the interior of the cottage to correspond in every respect with the outward appearance. The door entered into a portion appropriated to the winter reception of the cattle . . . from thence I passed directly into the kitchen, which was lighted by a sort of window; at the further end was a large chimney in which I observed a ladder which I concluded must lead to the bedchambers."

John Sweete's diary of 1797; description of a longhouse at Blackabrook.

The change from building in wood to stone took place in about the twelfth and thirteenth centuries. This period saw the beginning of our great cathedrals. Domestic stone buildings followed, and later, the longhouse of the established farmer.

Thus we find at the very centre of the Heathercombe estate, at the confluence of the Heathercombe stream and the central eastwards flowing tributary, straddling the Mariner's Way, the original medieval nucleus of the estate. This consisted of the two Dartmoor longhouses with extensive agricultural additions to the northern of the two (North Heathercombe), including a piggery in the rear yard, a substantial stock barn between the two houses, and a scattered series of smaller buildings. Nearby, some hundred metres downstream to the north, are the ruins of a corn mill.

North Heathercombe is now purely a dwelling house, three times as long as it is wide, with a porch and cross-passage slightly towards the lower (shippon) end. A single storey extension to the rear, extends to the length of the house and links with an extensive garden wall enclosing land to the front and lower end of the house, and possessing a series of six bee-boles at its junction with the western or upper end of the front elevation. The house walls appear to be of rendered granite rubble construction, with the chimney stacks also of granite: one centrally placed to the left above the cross-passage, and one set in the lower gable. The roof is thatched and hipped to the left.

+The defining factors of a longhouse in this situation being: commonality of entrance and occupation for people and animals, a cross-passage dividing the two areas, and a long axis set into the hill-slope, with the shippon at the lower end. For early occupation see Gill, 1970 – 174, also Devon Archaeology Issue No. 3, 1991. There are fewer than one hundred longhouses, even vaguely recognisable as such, and only about a quarter of these are more or less unaltered.

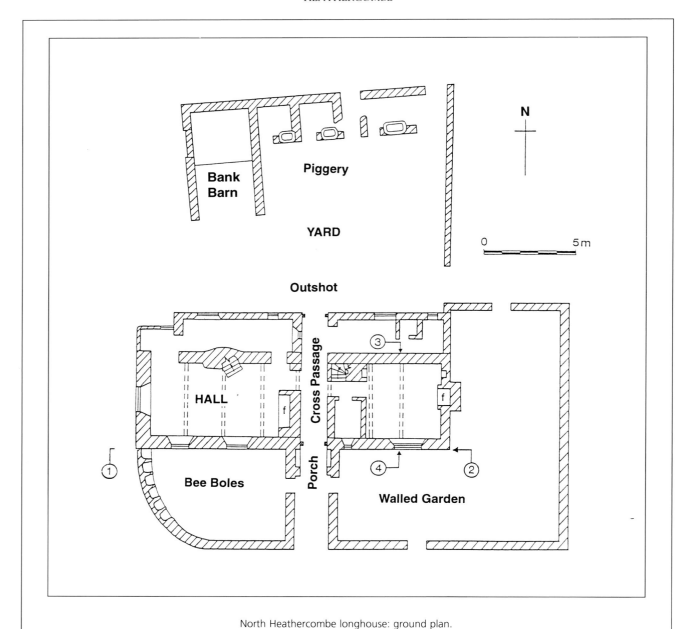

N

Bank
Barn

Piggery

YARD

0   5 m

Outshot

Cross Passage

HALL

f

Porch

③

f

②

①

Bee Boles

④

Walled Garden

North Heathercombe longhouse: ground plan.

SUGGESTED PHASING

Phase 1:

Fifteenth and early sixteenth centuries
Henry VII 1457 r. 1485– 1509
Henry VIII 1491 r. 1509– 1547

The earliest phase of North Heathercombe probably dates from the fifteenth or early sixteenth centuries and then consisted of the basic rectangular plan with an open hall above and shippon below the cross-passage. Subdivisions of this period were probably low timber plank and pillar partitions either side of an open hearth in the hall and in the cross-passage, the smoke rising to an open roof. The seven jointed-cruck roof-trusses that remain, albeit in a damaged condition today, could well be original, being of a face-pegged variety usually regarded as an early type. The spacing of the trusses from each end of the building indicate that the original configuration was of a fully hipped type with an end cruck springing directly from each gable.

Phase 2:

Late sixteenth century
Elizabeth I 1533 r. 1558– 1603

The next phase probably comprised the insertion of a closed truss between the hall and the inner room forming the bedchamber above the hall, accessed by a ladder stair. This truss, where visible, is of a square framed construction, characteristic of this period, with blades side-pegged to wall posts with a notched half-lap jointed collar beam and appears to underpin the earlier cruck assembly.

The Elizabethan Age created a rural prosperity, which continued through the sixteenth and seventeenth centuries, and saw substantial rebuilding of Devon Longhouses (Hayter Hames, 1981 p.85: Hoskins, 1953 p.265).

Phase 3:

Late seventeenth century
Charles II 1630 r.1660 – 85:
Mary 1662 r. 1689 – 94

This period is known as the period of great rebuilding. The increased farming wealth is conspicuously reflected in the buildings of the South West, and in particular, at North Heathercombe.

The hall fireplace, with its chamfered surround and corbelled lintel, both in massive dressed granite slabs, was constructed with its fireback forming part of an ashlar'd granite cross-passage wall, with its coved corbel course to support the ceiling beams over the passage.

The stair turret incorporating the stone circular staircase was inserted along the northern long wall, leading to the bedroom above. The room to the west remained open to the roof rafters.

It is not clear how much later the shippon end of the house was turned into living accommodation, with a separate wooden spiral staircase to the bedroom above, and a granite chimneystack providing fireplaces both in the lower room and the bedroom.

The conversion of the shippon must have been at a later date than the building of the fireplace and passage wall, but in the neighbouring Longhouse at Kendon, in the wall outside the entrance door, is the date 28 May 1675. Whether Heathercombe shippon was converted at the same time as Kendon, we do not know.

Phase 4:

The eighteenth century – The Georgian Period

Clearly, the major alterations at North Heathercombe took place between 1660 and the end of the next century, including the addition of the barn and the yard at the rear with its bank barn and piggery.

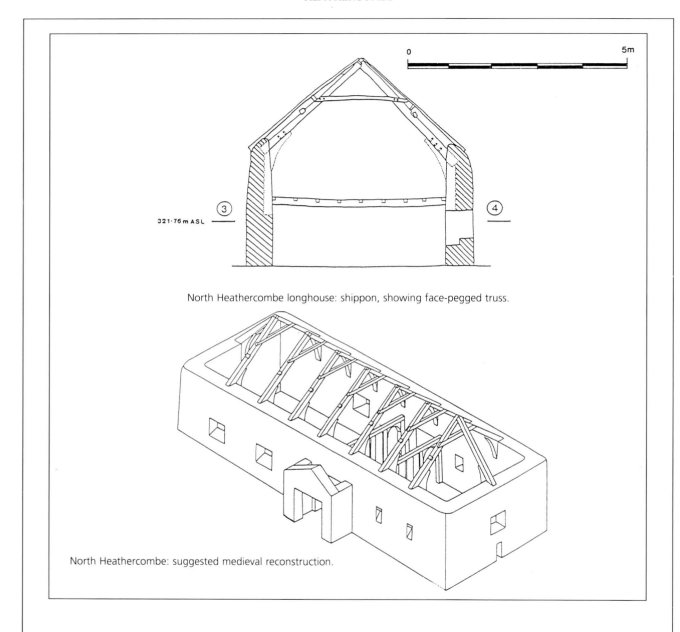

0   5m

321·76 m ASL

③   ④

North Heathercombe longhouse: shippon, showing face-pegged truss.

North Heathercombe: suggested medieval reconstruction.

Thus, by the end of the eighteenth century, the transformation of the longhouse, with its joint occupancy of men and animals, into a fully developed farmhouse was complete (Hayter Hames 1981 p.85; Stanes 1990, pp 41–43).

It is interesting to note that the bedrooms were inter-connected, with no privacy, and no doubt occupied partly by the family and partly by servants. Baring-Gould reported that in the traditional longhouse, the maidservants would sleep in the end room on one side of the house, and went to bed first, followed by the daughters of the house, who would sleep in the next room, then the menservants, and lastly, the master and mistress who slept in the master bedroom at the head of the stairs (Stanes 1990 p. 26).

It was only at a later stage that a passage was built along the backside of the longhouse, with doors to the bedrooms. At Heathercombe, such a passage was not constructed until Claude Pike modernised the house in 1967, when one of the bedrooms was turned into a bathroom and separate WC.

The addition of the porch may have been early in the eighteenth century, as at Lower Tar, Widecombe in 1707 (Hayward 1991; p. 471. Worth 1967; p. 44) or towards the end of the eighteenth century when Shapley had the addition of an elaborate porch in 1776 (Worth 1967 p. 411).

The semi-circular granite arch of the original doorway, typical of around Chagford and Widecombe (Worth 1967 p. 413) is to be found partly supporting garden gates on either side of the new porch, and partly supporting the entrance of the tunnel, permitting the stream to run under the courtyard.

Phase 5:

The nineteenth century

It was no doubt in the nineteenth century that the lean-to single storey addition was added to the rear of the house as a new diary, and later providing on the higher side a larder, kitchen and hot-water-cylinder cupboard, and on the lower side, a bathroom and WC (Worth 1967 p.410 and 413).

Phase 6:

The early twentieth century

In the early 1940s, Captain Evans took down the partition between the hall and the room to the west, and placed a ceiling in the room to the west, making a large bedroom as we see it today.

Alec Kitson, in the late 1940s, removed the ash house situated behind the piggeries, and built a shed in which he installed an electric generator. The National Electricity Grid came into the valley in 1963.

Phase 7:

In 1967/68, Claude Pike made substantial alterations, inserting a window in the west side of the hall, and a new access into the lean-to kitchen behind. The floor of the hall was lowered by about nine inches (23 cm). A window was put in the east side of the east bedroom. The small room of the cross-passage was equipped as a downstairs cloakroom.

The upstairs corridor, made between the east and west bedrooms, gave privacy to these bedrooms for the first time. One bedroom was turned into a bathroom with a separate WC. Central heating and modern lighting and plumbing was also installed. North Heathercombe became a listed building in 1991.

South Heathercombe

Although more comprehensively altered than its pair to the north, South Heathercombe also retains its early characteristics.

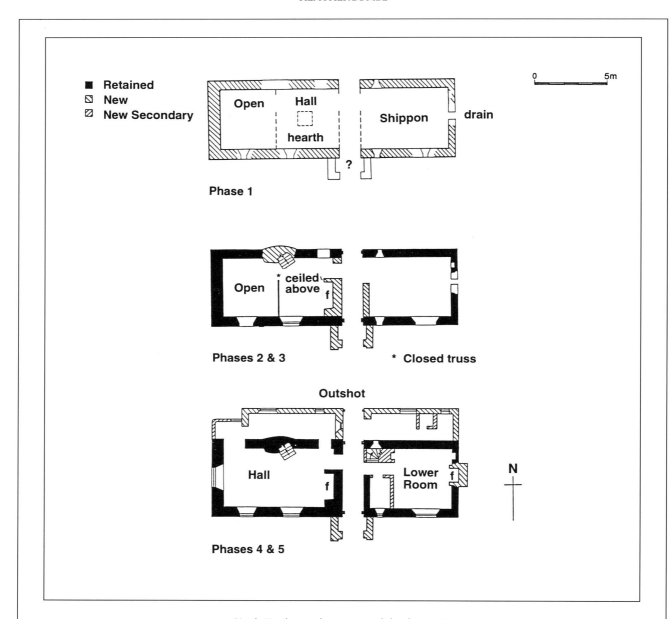

North Heathercombe: suggested development.

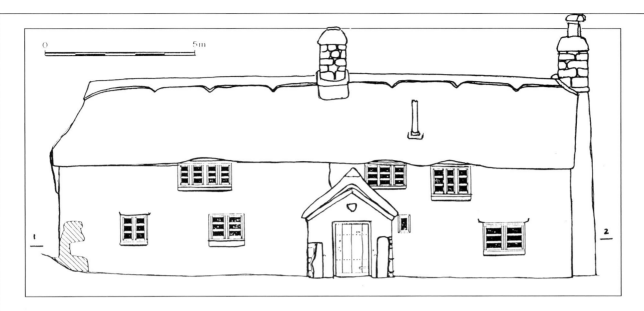

North Heathercombe: south elevation.

Inside it is almost identical to North Heathercombe, but the drop in the level from the cross-passage to the shippon is more noticeable. Regrettably, the early roof of North Heathercombe, with its cruck trusses and smoke-blackened thatch, is not parallel here, since a fire, not many years ago, totally destroyed any earlier timber.

The Coffin Hatch at North Heathercombe

The original staircase is a spiral stone staircase. A separate wooden staircase was subsequently installed in the eastern section, also spiral in construction. The spiral nature of the staircases resulted in there being in the main bedroom a coffin hatch – a section of the floor which can be lifted up to allow a coffin, or a large piece of furniture, to be taken to and from the first floor.

For very many years, coffins of the dead in the Forest of Dartmoor proper had to be taken overland to Lydford, although, at a later date, concession was given for coffins to be taken to Widecombe.

It is suspected that the dead from Heathercombe had to be taken down the valley and across along the church path, past Langdon to North Bovey.

HEATHERCOMBE TITHES

At the time when the 1842 Tithe Map was prepared, the land at Heathercombe was paying tithe to the Vicar of Widecombe, and tithes of corn and grain to the Dean and Chapter of Salisbury Cathedral. The subsequent tithe rent charges on the land were redeemed when Claude Pike purchased the land now comprising the Heathercombe estate.

An endeavour has been made to discover how these tithes originated, and why some were paid to the Dean and Chapter of Salisbury, by tracing the development of Christianity in England and the resulting evolution of the church tithe. At the same time, it was realised that there may be a link between the Heathercombe tithe and the royalties paid on the clay worked in the Bovey Basin, also to the Dean and Chapter of Salisbury in support of the Teignton Regis Prebend.

The Development of Christianity in England

Little is known of the pre-Christian religion in Great Britain (Costen 1992; 42).

Christianity spread throughout Europe soon after the Edict of Tolerance in 313, when it was recognised by the Roman Emperor, Constantine. It was, however, also in part developed in Celtic Britain by groups of clergy, some inspired by St Patrick and St Columba. They established churches and lived communally. These churches were called minsters and were situated in different parts of the country, with no particular territorial boundaries. A minster was established at Exeter. Through these minsters a Celtic Christian tradition developed, associated with the numerous Celtic saints; for example, in Cornwall St Endelienta of St Endellion and St Petroc of Padstow (Mildren, 1988; 44).

When the Saxons entered Devon in the seventh century, having been converted to Christianity, they continued the establishment of minsters, but their tradition was Roman, thanks to the teachings of St Augustine sent to England in 597 by Pope Gregory.

Aethelbert of Kent, in about 600, was the first English king to become Christian.

Theodore of Tarsus, Archbishop from 669 to 690, brought all the Saxon minsters under Canterbury. He established some fourteen as bishoprics, with fixed territorial sees.

The Celtic Christian (Orme 1991; 6) however, regarded the Christians of the Roman tradition as alien Christians (Orme 1991, and Mildren 1988; 50).

Along with the minsters, a number of other religious sites existed from early times. These were often burial grounds on which a church had

developed once there was Christian funerals at which Christian prayers were said. The churches at Manaton and Widecombe may have developed in this way – Widecombe certainly believes this to have been the case – but there is no documentary evidence of this type of church in Devon until the eve of the Norman Conquest.

By the Norman Conquest, the division of the country into parishes, and the establishment of larger districts of local government, known as hundreds, had taken place. The hundreds first appeared in the reign of Edmund, 939 – 941 (Hoskins 1953; 50).

After the Norman Conquest, Lanfranc became Archbishop of Canterbury in 1070, and many abbots were replaced with Continental clergy, which caused resentment by abandoning the observance of some local saints (Stenton 1990; 672).

The Development of Tithes

The minsters provided spiritual services to the laity – masses, baptisms, confessions, prayers and funerals. In return, the people were expected to look to the nearest minster for these services, and to support it with donations of food and money. These payments, originally, were, at the donor's choice, to pilgrims or to the poor of the parish. But early in the eighth century, we find King Ine, King of the West Saxons; ordering his subjects to pay Church Scot – a payment in kind, e.g. grain – once a year on St Martin's Day.

It was only by degrees that the tithe came to replace the Church Scot. In the seventh century, payment was still only a matter of conscience (Stenton 1990; 154). In the decree by a synod held in 786, the payment of tithes, in general, was strongly enjoined.

King Edgar (959 – 975) in 962, went further and appropriated the tithes to minsters, and later, to other churches. The development of tithes – one-tenth of crops and animals – paid each year was of immense importance to church history. It enabled the system of small local churches, with resident clergy, to grow up. The right of tithes had been fully established by the Norman Conquest, and for the next nine hundred years, provided the main support of the clergy. After the Norman Conquest, many of the minsters became simple parish churches, losing their surplus clergy.

The churches of Manaton and Widecombe did not exist at the time of the Norman Conquest (History of the Diocese of Exeter). They were, however, receiving tithes in the early part of the thirteenth century. Teignmouth and Exminster are the only churches mentioned in the Exeter Domesday (Fisher, 1962; 387).

How the Dean and Chapter of Salisbury Became Entitled to Dues from Land in Devon (including Heathercombe)

In AD 703, King Ine of the West Saxons, established a new Bishop's Seat at Sherborne to supervise the church in the lands which the Saxons had recently conquered west of Selwood, in Somerset, Dorset and Devon.

In 739, a charter of King Aethelherd of Wessex gave to Crediton Minster, founded in 705, a vast area of land, including land in the Drewsteignton region, probably including Manaton, Widecombe and Heathercombe (see also the Paedington Charter and Gill, 1970). As Crediton was under Sherborne, this gave the Bishop of Sherborne land and a base in Devon.

Late in the ninth century King Alfred (848, r.871 – 900) gave to his friend, the Welsh Bishop Asser, what Asser described as 'Exeter with all the districts belonging to it in Devon and Cornwall'. This, generally, is interpreted as making Asser a suffragan bishop, auxiliary to the Bishop of Sherborne (Orme, 1992; 19).

The See of Salisbury was founded by the Council of London in 1075, being removed from Sherborne, it being ordained that bishops' sees should be removed from obscure places to a town (Stenton 1990; 666).

In the Foundation Charter of 1091, Bishop Osmond of Salisbury declared that Salisbury had been granted in perpetuity, amongst other properties, 'the Church of Sherborne, together with the entire tithe of the vill, and other appurtenances'. (Salisbury Archives and Stenton). Salisbury thus acquired the right to tithes from land in Devon.

Bishopric of Devon

When Bishop Asser died in 909, the South West was divided from Sherborne permanently, and a new Bishop's Seat was founded at Crediton, with the Bishop being responsible for both Devon and Cornwall. This bishopric was not very well endowed (Orme 1991; 20), Sherborne no doubt retaining most of its tithes on land in Devon, in spite of what Finberg writes (Finberg 1969; 34), where he indicates that the new Bishop of Devon was wealthy.

In 930, it is known that King Athelston (924 – 940) gave Exeter Minster lands and relics, and established a Bishop's See at St Germans in Cornwall.

In the year 1027, the bishoprics of Crediton and St Germans were held in plurality. Leofric became joint Bishop in 1036, but he gained a poor opinion of the standards of discipline of the Crediton canons, and disliked having his cathedral at Crediton in the countryside, and wished to move it to Exeter, a fortified city of growing importance.

In 1050, he applied to the Pope for permission to move his cathedral to Exeter (Stenton 1990; 666). As a result, Pope Leo IX wrote to King Edward The Confessor ordering the move, and at the same time, approving the union of the two diocese. Leofric elected the old minster in Exeter as his new Cathedral.

Disputes over the payment of Tithes and Dues to the Dean and Chapter of Salisbury and the Rectors of Manaton and Widecombe

The archives of the Dean and Chapter of Salisbury reveal that in the thirteenth century, there were a number of disputes concerning the payment of tithes

Manaton church.

to the Dean and Chapter of Salisbury, involving the Dean and Chapter of Exeter and the Rectors of North Bovey, Manaton and Widecombe. For example, on 13 November, 1274, the Rector of Manaton and the Rector of North Bovey recognised the Dean and Chapter of Salisbury's right to the tithes they had received, and agreed to repay what they had received by way of instalments.

Again, on 2 November, 1281, it was recorded that there were disputes with regard to the tithes at Chalvecomb (Challacombe), Soneston (Soussons) and Hevetre (Hevitree), and that proof was offered supporting the Dean and Chapter of Salisbury's claim by virtue of an ordinance of William, the late Bishop of Exeter, and confirmed by Pope Innocent IV.

Again, on 1 October, 1283, the Bishop of Exeter ordered the Dean of Moreton to restore to the Dean and Chapter of Salisbury the tithes of sheaves of Chalvecomb and Manaton, which had been claimed by John, the Rector of Widecombe.

Again, on 14 August, 1476, there was an agreement between the Dean and Chapter of Salisbury with Peter, the Rector of Manaton, and Peter, the Rector of North Bovey, concerning the tithes and profits of Hevetre. They acknowledged the right of the Dean and Chapter of Salisbury to these tithes and profits, and agreed to pay arrears.

The following is an example of how other charges on land arose (Exeter Cathedral Archives 1934 – 1937):

In 1283, Ralph le Rus (Rous), son of Richard, sold to Sir Roger le Rus one acre and the advowson of the Church of Widecombe, with the Manor of Widecombe.

Sir Roger le Rus then sold the land and advowson of the Church of Widecombe to the Dean and Chapter of Exeter. The Dean and Chapter then entered into a bond to pay 10 silver Marks yearly towards the stipend of a Chaplain to perform the obit of Roger de Toriz, the fourth Dean of Exeter (1268–74). Sir Roger le Rus, who was Roger de Toriz's executor – and no doubt friend – must have arranged this and charged the performance of the obit to the Church of Widecombe, the obit to be celebrated at the altar of St Richard and Radegund in the Church of Exeter where Roger de Toriz is buried (see Dymond–*Widecombe in the Moor*).

Peter Quinil, Bishop of Exeter (1280 – 1291) in 1283, confirmed the appointment of the Church of Widecombe to perform the orbit of Richard de Torres.

In 1285, a royal licence was granted assigning the Church of Widecombe to the Dean and Chapter of Exeter—the incumbents of Widecombe from that time were vicars. The Dean and Chapter of Exeter kept the Rectorial tithe, but the incumbents of Widecombe were allowed the Vicarial tithe, part of

The church and village of Widecombe.

Widecombe church.

which was thereafter paid by the owners of Heathercombe (*Archives of the Dean and Chapter of Exeter*).

Heathercombe Tithes

At the time when the 1842 Tithe Map was prepared, the land at Heathercombe was paying £3.5s. per annum tithe to the Vicar of Widecombe, and £3.10s. for the tithes of corn and grain to the Dean and Chapter of Salisbury. The subsequent rent charges on the land were redeemed when Claude Pike purchased the land now comprising the Heathercombe estate.

Conclusion

It would appear that the tithe of £3.10s. payable to the Dean and Chapter of Salisbury was based on that very early land ownership in Devon, and the tithe of £3.5s. to the Vicar of Widecombe was based on the general liability to pay tithe, although why it was paid to Widecombe, rather than Manaton, is as yet not clear.

Teignton Regis – Salisbury Cathedral Prebend

Similar to the payment of a tithe by the Heathercombe estate to the Dean and Chapter of

Salisbury Cathedral, Watts, Blake, Bearne & Company Plc have for many years, until quite recently, paid royalties on the clay they had produced on the Church Commissioners Preston Manor estate, in support of the Teignton Regis Prebend of Salisbury Cathedral. Research has been undertaken to discover how this had arisen.

Hoskins, 1954, (p.421) has indicated that Kingsteignton has a long history. It was one of the early villages in the Saxon Conquest, founded probably about 700, or shortly afterwards, and was the head of a vast royal estate centred on the Teign estuary (Devon Archaeological Society No. 45, 1987 (p.75).

Few writers seem to have appreciated the importance of Kingsteignton in the early medieval period. It has, however, now been concluded that Kingsteignton had been the head of a Saxon royal estate, the Saxon estate having been large, including Moretonhampstead, North Bovey, Manaton and Lustleigh to the North. Whether this was the same land that King Aethelherd, in 739, gave to Crediton Minster, being a large part of the Teignton Hundred, we do not know, but just as the boundaries of King Aethelherd's grant are uncertain, so are the boundaries of the medieval Teignbridge Hundred. In 1333, they were defined as containing, amongst others, Bovey Tracey, Kingsteignton, Teigngrace, Ilsington, Ashburton, Manaton, North Bovey, Moretonhampstead and Lustleigh.

King Aethelherd's grant of land to Crediton Minster, which was under the Bishop of Sherborne, meant that when Sherborne was transferred to the See of Salisbury in 1075, Bishop Osmond of Salisbury could record that amongst other properties, Salisbury had been granted in perpetuity 'the Church of Sherborne, together with the entire tithe of the vill and other appurtenances' (*Salisbury Archives* and Stenton, 1990; 666).

It is clear that in this way, the Dean and Chapter acquired the right to tithe, and other dues not only in Kingsteignton, but to a large area to the north – hence the Heathercombe tithe.

It was the charter of the time of Bishop Roger, confirmed in 1146 by Pope Eugenius, which gave the property of the Church of Teignton to constitute a Prebend of Salisbury Cathedral. The manor of Preston, Kingsteignton, on which clay was discovered, claimed royalties on the clay for the benefit of the Prebend. These royalties ceased in about 1970 when the Church Commissioners sold the land to Watts, Blake, Bearne & Company Limited.

The Paedington Charter

As has been indicated, the exact extent of the land included in King Aethelherd's grant, and in the Teignbridge Hundred, is uncertain, no documentary evidence being available. There is, however, one document – the Paedington Charter – which defines the land, the subject of the charter. This charter covered as extensive area of land, including the modern parishes of Widecombe, Manaton, Ilsington and Ashburton (see Map 14 and Map 15, and the table showing the bound points of this charter, near Heathercombe).

It is believed that the Paedington Charter must have been the confirmation of a much older charter, for the Domesday Book does not recognise it in the schedules of land under Hundreds which have different boundaries (see Plan on p.78 of *Devon Archaeological Proceedings* No.45; and *Devon Archaeology* p.18).

Because of the disturbed times in the two or three centuries before the Norman Conquest, grants made by one king might frequently have to be confirmed in a subsequent reign (Gill, 1970 p.77).

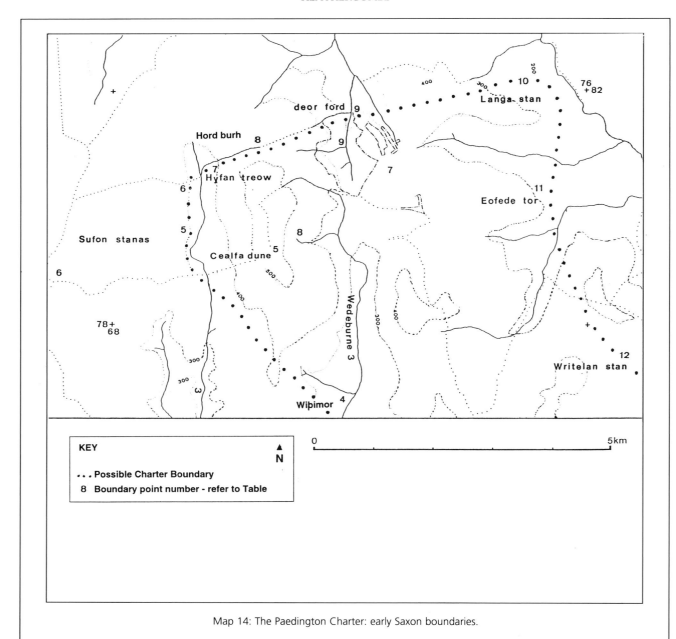

Map 14: The Paedington Charter: early Saxon boundaries.

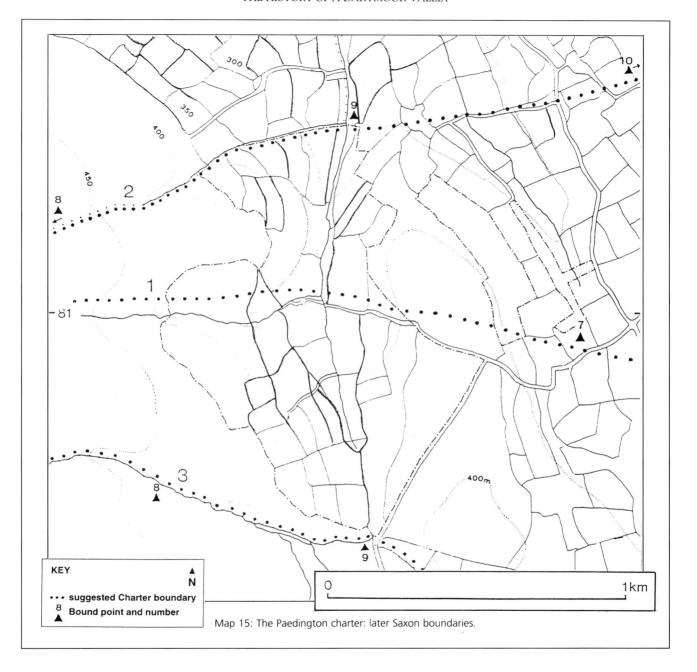

KEY

▲
N

••• suggested Charter boundary

8
▲ Bound point and number

Map 15: The Paedington charter: later Saxon boundaries.

Table to Map Charter Bound Points	Route		
	1	2	3
7	Heofan treow (Heatree)	–	–
8	–	Hord burh (Grimspound)	Bury Pound
9	–	deor ford (deer ford)	ford
10	–	langa stan (long stone) -	

Route 1 is the previously accepted version first described in the E.P.N.S series (Devon vol II; pp.461–2) and routes 2 and 3 alternative versions.

THE 1842 TITHE MAP SURVEY AND APPORTIONMENT

Whereas an Award of Rent Charge in lieu of TITHES in the Parish of Manaton in the County of Devon was, on the fifth day of March in the Year of our Lord One Thousand Eight Hundred and Forty Two confirmed by the Tithe Commissioners for England and Wales of which Award with the Schedule therein comprised the following is a Copy:-
Know all Men by these Presents . . .

Introduction to the Manaton Tithe Map 1842–3.

The greatest census in England since Domesday took place in the 1840s when a survey was undertaken parish by parish of the whole of the country. There were two main reasons for the survey: one, to ascertain the extent of the Church's rent-charges in lieu of tithes from the land in what was to become a long running dispute with the landowners; and secondly, accurately to record the nation's wealth in terms of agricultural production.

Heathercombe is, of course, included in the Manaton Parish Survey of 1842 – 3, copies of which are now lodged at Exeter and London, and it is from the London copy (Public Records Office IR29/9/271) that the following information has been retrieved:

In total, Manaton Parish comprised an area of some 4201 acres (1700 ha) excluding glebe land, over half of which was common or moor: 2243 acres (908 ha); 220 acres (91 ha) furzeland, and the rest, some 479 acres (194 ha) divided between meadow and pasture, plantation, woodland and orchards or gardens.

Heathercombe was somewhat smaller than the present estate, with most of the north-eastern corner belonging to Vogwell Farm, and totalled an area of 159 acres (64 ha) sub-divided into 55 separate fields or plots. It is unfortunate that the column in the Apportionment Register that normally details the

613	Lenhay & Court					
614	Lower Burrows	3	1	30		
617	Little Plot		1	50		
618	House & Garden			2?		
619	Plantation			1K		
620	Grassy close plantation			16		
621	Grassy close	2	3			
		78	1	83	√	3	10

Hether Combes

88	Broad park Brake	6	2	26
89	Higher Broad park	2	2	34
90	Middle Broadpark	2	1	32
91	Lower Broadpark	3	1	36
92	Higher Moor	1	1	6
93	Lower park	3		6
94	Lower Moor	2		9
351	Mill Meadow	1		1
352	Willow Plot			8
354	Crockhill plantation		2	37
355	Mill ware	2	2	12
356	Homer Long Graze	1	3	20
357	Yonder Long Graze	2		20
358	Higher Long graze	2	1	29
359	Higher Hill Broke	2	2	12

Detail from the original Tithe Apportionment document, 1842.

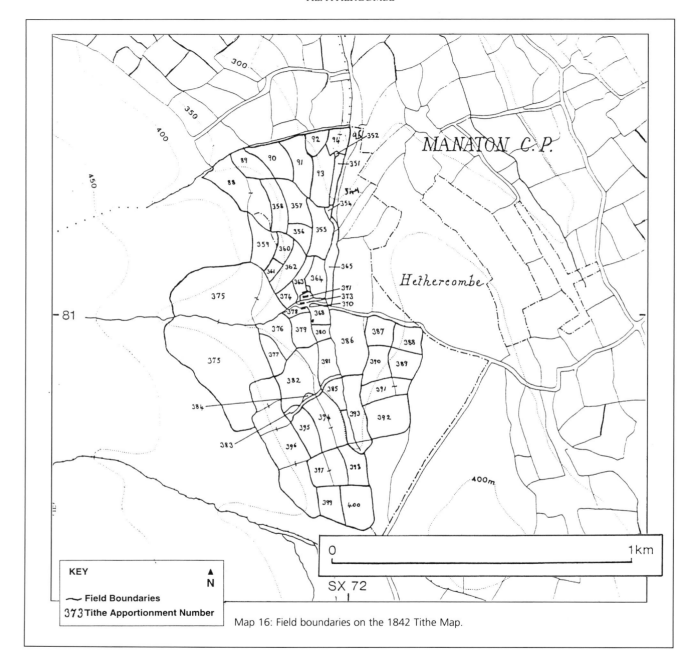

Map 16: Field boundaries on the 1842 Tithe Map.

The 1843 Tithe Map and Apportionment

North and South Heathercombe were owned and occupied by John Pethybridge.

Field name Table (see Map 16)

88 Broad Park Brake	383 Watering Place	362 Lower Hill
90 Middle Broad Park	385 Heathercombe Moor	364 Back Meadow
92 Higher Moor	387 Water Park	368 Little Meadow
94 Lower Moor	389 Rock Park	371 House Road
352 Willow Plat	391 Homer Eastern Close	374 Orchard
355 Mill Ware	393 Higher Long Piece	376 Stainty Park
357 Yonder Long Graze	395 Higher Long Piece	378 Hay
359 Higher Hill Brake	397 Higher Cleave	380 Middle Meadow
361 Little Hill	399 Higher Hewstone Park	382 Dunnicks Field
363 Little Close	89 Higher Broad Park	384 Garden Copse
365(A) Coombe (Ruins of Mill)	91 Lower Broad Park	386 and Road
370 House and Homestead	93 Lower Park	388 Ludgate Close
373 Garden	351 Mill Meadow	390 Broad Piece
375 Newtake	354 Crockhill Plantation	392 Yonder Eastern Close
377 Waste	356 Homer Long Graze	396 Furzey Ground
379 Shute Park	358 Higher Long Graze	398 Lower Cleave
381 Higher Meadow	360 Higher Hill	400 Lower Hewstone Park

Vogwell was owned and occupied by Thomas Pethybridge.

349 Mill Pits
95 Pitts
96 Pitty Park

'state of cultivation' is blank in the case of this survey, and the proportion of land put down to any one use cannot be ascertained accurately.

Of some further interest, neighbouring Vogwell has three field-names, indicating possible tin-mining (Pitts, Pitty Park and Mill Pits) and a field adjacent to some prehistoric hut circles called Yelland, usually a derivation of 'old lands', indicating early cultivation. A field just to the east of Heathercombe settlement is called 'Further Hether Comb', which presumably once belonged to the main estate, and may denote a certain fluidity of ownership.

JAY'S GRAVE – A DARTMOOR LEGEND

Kitty Jay is said to have been a young, unmarried housemaid at Ford Farm, where she was seduced by a young farm labourer. Relentlessly persecuted by her employers when her plight became obvious, she went out and hanged herself in one of the barns on Canna Farm. As a suicide, she was denied burial in any of the neighbouring churchyards, and was interred at the wayside spot where the three parishes of Manaton, North Bovey and Widecombe meet.

About 1860, James Bryant, then the owner of Hedge Barton, determined to ascertain the truth, had the grave excavated. Inside were found the skull and bones, pronounced by pathologists to be those of a young female. Bryant had the remains placed in a wooden box, reinterred on the same spot, and a small mound raised above–as it is today. The actual date of death is not known, but is presumed to be in the eighteenth century.

Nobody knows who places the flowers on this grave – very often wild flowers – but very rarely can the grave been seen without such flowers (*Crossing, 1912 295 and St Leger-Gordon, 115*).

In June, 1979, the BBC asked for the removal of the fences round Jay's Grave, for they wanted to film it in connection with a programme to be called 'Leap in the Dark'. This featured a girl in Liverpool being hypnotised, and under hypnosis, describing the story of an earlier life, referring to Manaton and Chagford, it having been discovered that this was the same as the legend of Kitty Jay. It was emphatically confirmed by the BBC that neither the hypnotist nor the girl knew of the legend, and of the tradition of flowers being invariably placed on the grave.

Jay's Grave.

THE MARINER'S WAY

Crossing Devon – The Seafaring County

The Mariner's Way is first described by Crossing in his *Guide to Dartmoor* (page 65) as an ancient way from Bideford to Dartmouth. It is said that it was once used by sailors passing from one of these ports to the other. At intervals of about eight or ten miles, there were resthouses with accommodation (Hayward 1991 30). The route approached the moor through Throwleigh, Gidleigh, Teigncombe, Frenchbere, Shapley Coombe – where it runs through a passage of a dwelling house – Shapley, Hookney, Kendon, Heathercombe, Natsworthy Gate, to Widecombe.

It is said that in medieval times, seafaring men who had been paid off at one or other of the North Devon ports, were in the habit of making their way across the county to Dartmouth, or some other port on the south coast, in search of a new berth, traversing The Mariner's Way. This tradition is supported by a number of entries in the Gidleigh Church records, between 1730 and 1774, recording the giving of alms to sailors (Starkey, 1983; 147: Gill, 1970; 193 and Hemery, 1986; 21–39).

FARMING IN THE HEATHERCOMBE VALLEY SINCE THE STONE AGE

In the early Stone Age, the inhabitants of Dartmoor were hunter gatherers moving around in nomadic bands, living on the fruits of the forest, game and fish from the river.

The Neolithic, or New Stone Age (about 4000 BC to 2000 BC), saw the beginnings of the agricultural clearance of trees and scrub in order to cultivate the first cereal crops–a primitive form of wheat.

The Bronze Age (c.2000–600 BC) because of a much warmer climate, saw a still greater clearance of trees from the higher ground. In consequence, by the late Bronze Age, a way of life based chiefly on arable farming had been achieved (see under Bronze Age p.16). There followed several centuries of intensive pastural and arable husbandry, largely eliminating the forest cover of the higher ground. During this period, the Heathercombe valley had a substantial population as is proved by the numerous hut circles and reaves.

By the end of the Bronze Age, however (about 600 BC) consequent upon a dramatic deterioration of the climate as a result of colder and wetter conditions, the moor gradually became depopulated.

From this time, until the arrival of the Saxons, there is no evidence, at present, of settled habitation on Dartmoor, although small groups of people may well have remained around the edges of the moor. During this period, at lower land levels, the Iron Age men, with their axes, cleared some of the lower-lying forests, moving to the richer soils.

When the Saxons arrived in Devon in the seventh century, they too preferred the lower land between 500ft and 1000ft. But as the climate again improved, they gradually moved towards the higher ground, which by the ninth century had become a hunting ground for the Wessex kings, and on which the farms below had acquired common rights. It must be during this period that the Heathercombe valley became re-inhabited, and the clearance of trees completed. There is clear indication of the cultivation in the surrounding valleys, particularly noticeable in the Challacombe valley. The Domesday Survey of 1086 indicates that farming on a substantial scale had taken place for a considerable time in the past in Bovey Tracey, North Bovey, Manaton, Shapley, Natsworthy and Bag Tor, and, in consequence, presumably also at Heathercombe, being a sheltered valley in the middle. Heathercombe is not mentioned in Domesday, along with many other farmsteads and hamlets. Its omission, therefore, does

'Lazybeds', evidence of early cultivation in the Challacombe Valley.

not mean it was uninhabited (Hoskins 1953; 58 and 69). Hoskins (p.55) records that by the eleventh century, farming was taking place up to the 1000–1200ft level). Heathercombe is first documented as Heddercombe in 1244 (Gover et al. 1931–2; 482).

Farming at Heathercombe would not have been adversely affected in the eleventh century by the Norman Conquest. The following two centuries were periods of expansion (Costen 1992; 33) only to be halted in the fourteenth century by another deterioration of climate, a series of bad harvests and in 1348, the Black Death. The Black Death, which killed about one-third of the population, probably had a seriously adverse effect on Heathercombe; it certainly had on tin streaming (Harris 1968;19).

The devastating effect of the Black Death in the neighbourhood is demonstrated by the fact that the churches of Bovey Tracey, Lustleigh, Manaton, North Bovey and Widecombe all lost their encumbents (*History of the Diocese of Exeter* p.248).

We have records that Heathercombe was paying tithes in the thirteenth century to the parish of Widecombe and to the Dean and Chapter of Salisbury, reference being made to tithes of corn. At that time, corn clearly was a significant crop.

It is not known when the corn mill in the valley was built. Its location was no doubt determined by the head of water available for the overshot wheel. Domesday Book shows that England was covered by mills of that kind at the time of the Norman Conquest.

One of the two millstones found at Heathercombe.

The existence of a mill at Heathercombe is confirmed by the two mill stones, and the configuration of the site, the bank for the leat to feed the overshot wheel, and the tailrace. It was speculated that because of the tin streaming in the valley it might have been a tin mill. Dr Greeves has stated that this is clearly not the case. He believes that the mill is of the early nineteenth century, as it was not marked on the Ordnance Surveyor's drawings of 1802–3, and he feels, therefore, that the mill was built some time between 1803 and 1828. On the other hand, the 1842 Tithe Map describes the site as 'ruins of a mill'; and in the Devon Record Office there is a draft Assignment dated 12 November, 1828, between B. Stanbury and Robert Tucker to Henry Ferris of Heathercombe West Mills in Manaton, of the remainder of a term of ninety-nine years. It does not say when the term commenced.

It is, in consequence, felt that the mill is much older. Hayter Hames, 1991, refers to much older corn mills in the district, and it is conjectured that the mill was probably in operation, as other mills, in the seventeenth and eighteenth centuries, when the longhouses were being fully developed, at a time of general prosperity.

Tin streaming in the valley was already at its height during this period. All this activity was no doubt the basis of prosperity in the valley, and in consequence, brought about the subsequent improvement of the accommodation in the longhouses. It would seem, therefore, that from the late Saxon times there has been continuous farming in the valley, some arable, some pasture, with common rights held on parts of Dartmoor.

By the end of the nineteenth century farming had become mostly pastural, rather than arable, relying mainly on sheep, pigs and cattle, with a little arable for winter feed.

Although there was some tree planting at the end of the nineteenth, and the early part of the twentieth centuries, the low lying fields were still mainly pasture. This changed in 1949, when they were dedicated for forestry, and in due course planted with conifers, hence the abandonment of agriculture in the valley, except for two paddocks adjoining North and South Heathercombe, and the open Vogwell and Heatree Downs.

The Newtake Wall Builders

There are medieval newtake walls on the estate. The first thing the early Dartmoor settler had to do was to enclose the land he had marked out and, consequently, the building of a wall was an occupation which preceded all other forms of labour. When more land was enclosed, of course, more walls were required, and thus the construction of walls became one of the Dartmoor settlers' crafts. The making of the enclosures had many names: one that has survived is that of newtake. An age old forest custom allowed the occupants of the ancient tenements to enclose up to 8 acres of moor each time a new tenant entered a farm. For this they paid 1 1/2d an acre to the Duchy of Cornwall. The pace of enclosing newtakes increased towards the end of the eighteenth century. The large Heathercombe newtake was probably enclosed about that time. The walls were usually about 4ft high and built from stones at hand, often with daylight seen through them.

One of the newtake walls at Heathercombe.

The building of the walls was achieved through the skilled use of the crow-bar, the stones often being conveyed to the required spot by a sledge pulled by a pony or horse (Crossing, 1966; 34).

Common Rights on Hameldown

It is quite clear that common rights on Hameldown and Challacombe Down had been acquired and attached to the land in medieval times, and were exercised right up to the middle of the twentieth century – the principal right being that of pasture. This right has been registered for Heathercombe under the Commons Registration Act of 1965 (Ref.209/D/308 and 399 CL.109) for 200 sheep, 50 cattle and 10 ponies in respect of North and South Heathercombe farms. No common of piscary or 'to stray' was granted. The common of turbery (to take turf or peat) was not claimed, there being no evidence of this common having been exercised on Hameldown by Heathercombe tenants.

As there was no common right of turbery, and as there is no indication that turf or peat has been taken from Hameldown, the only other source of fuel for the occupants of North and South Heathercombe must have been wood. One must therefore speculate that wood for fuel was taken from land not arable or pasture. This would be land up the valley to Hameldown, and along the sides of the Heathercombe Brook, including land destroyed by tin streaming. Oak, Ash and Beech from the hedgerows may also have been used, although one has to bear in mind that most of the hedges were stone walls, unlike those in the lowlands.

The Evolution of the Field Gate

Slot-and-L Gates

The distribution of these gates is most frequent on the east side of Dartmoor–in Widecombe, Manaton, North Bovey and Moretonhampstead parishes. (Worth 1967; 364 and Challacombe Survey).

Slot and 'L' gateposts (left), swinging gate (right).

Bee boles at Ford Farm.

Early Swinging Gates

The Rev. S. Rowe, writing from personal observations in 1848 says: 'The primitive contrivance for hanging gates of the Moorland crofts and commons may be seen employed in the neighbourhood of Chagford. No iron hinge of any kind, nor gate post, is employed. An oblong moor stone block, in which a socket is drilled, is built into the wall from which it projects sufficiently to receive the back stanchion of the gate, while a corresponding socket is sunk in a similar stone fixed to the ground below'. (Worth, 1967; 358)

Both these types of gate can be found on the Heathercombe estate.

Bee Boles

Until the middle of the last century, in the wetter and windier parts of Britain, bee keepers frequently kept their beehives, or skeps, in bee boles. These bee boles were recesses built in walls specifically for this purpose.

There are six bee boles in the wall of the small enclosed garden to the left of the front door of North Heathercombe (see page 81). These recesses are the usual size 15 inches x 12 inches (380mm x 305mm) size and face south-east, so that the bees would be warmed by the morning sun. The base of the bee boles is 2ft (610mm) from the ground, a convenient height for working, although the skeps were rarely handled, except when the honeycombs were harvested from them.

Bee boles seem to be a speciality of Britain and are found in many counties, with a considerable number in Devon; for example, at Ford Farm, Manaton; Bickington and Buckfast Abbey. Manaton is mentioned in Domesday as the only manor in Devon keeping bees for honey (Risdon, 1992; 10)

THE HISTORY OF TREES AT HEATHERCOMBE FROM PRE-GLACIAL TIMES

It had been said that hills and trees and streams are the warp of Nature's pattern of beauty, and that the weft is woven by the shuttle of light.

(Rogers, 1942;2)

The Bovey Basin Lignite Deposits

The Bovey Basin clay was deposited in that part of the Tertiary Period, known as late Eocene and early Oligocene, between thirty-eight million and twenty-eight million years ago. These deposits were washed down from the granite mass of Dartmoor to the north and in part, from the slates of the Culm Measures.

The layers of clay and sandy material were interspersed with vegetation. From the plant remains, pollen and spores, the nature of the vegetation resulting in the lignite formation has been assessed. The layers of clay, sand and vegetation were deposited in shallow lakes which formed intermittently on the broad valley floor.

The climate at the time was sub-tropical, and as far as trees are concerned, as distinct from ferns and mosses, the lignites were derived from, in the main, *Sequoia Couttsiae* (Elwes and Henry, 1913; 687, Vol.III) but also *Carpinus, Boveyanus, Fargus Minima, Zelkova Boveyana, Magnolia Boveyana, Cinnamomum, Tilia* and *Nyssa* (Chandler, 1957). The trees probably covered the valley slopes and were washed into the adjacent valley as debris during periods of flood.

In the millions of years between then and the last great Ice Age, the climate and vegetation have changed dramatically, the ice-cap pushing the sub-tropical and temperate flora further and further south, only partially to return gradually as the last Ice Age retreated.

Since the Last Ice Age

During the height of the Pleistocene Ice Ages, which began about two million years ago, most of England north of Dartmoor lay below glaciers, effectively blotting out all vegetation. Towards the end of this period, between about 20 000 and 15 000 BC, there followed a succession of post-glacial climatic phases. During the first ten thousand years, between 20 000 and 10 000 BC, there was a period of slow warming of the earth, the ice retreating and the land surface being invaded and colonised by plants, typical of the arctic tundras. There was no true forest cover, although several of the dwarf willows and dwarf birch became abundant. The few human inhabitants were Paleolithic men, living by fishing, hunting and food-gathering.

Around 10 000 BC, the temperature again dropped a little, reaching a low point around 8800 BC, after which it started to rise again.

The next period–the Boreal period–commencing about 7000 BC, was one of a warmer climate, which saw the return to Britain of great forests from the European continent to which Britain was still attached. This lasted until about 5000 BC. Of the invading trees first came the birches on the edges of the tundra, followed by Scots pine. Hazel also spread quickly on the edge of the pine forests. Mixed oak forests then began to be established, containing elm, ash, lime, rowan, hawthorn, and juniper, with alder in the wetter sites. Rackman, 1986, believes that some woods were dominated by small-leaved lime.

In due course, the warmer and more humid conditions encouraged the formation of moss and other peat-forming plants, which checked the regeneration of pine. By the time of the 'climatic optimum', around about 5000 BC, the pine woods would largely have been replaced by mixed oak wood, further encouraged during the warm, humid conditions of the Atlantic period (4000 to 2500 BC). During this period–the New Stone Age–Neolithic men began to have the first real effect on the woodlands scene.

It is thought that pine would have been completely eliminated by the end of the period, about 600 BC, except perhaps on valley knolls, and that beech was first recorded in the south-west of England, although in the Dartmoor area all the beech appear to have been planted by man, perhaps as late as the seventeenth century. Ash is a true native and would have come in with the first wave of oak woods.

On a visit to Zermatt in July, 1992, the author was interested to note that above the 9000ft contour, and just below the glaciers, vegetation above the tree line included dwarf alder, willow, alpenrose (*Rhododendron Ferrugineum*) and prostrate juniper. The soil was too acid for birch.

The trees on the tree line were Arola pine (*Pinus Cembra*) Scots pine, white fir, rowan and a substantial amount of larch (*Larix Decidua*).

It is surprising that Norway Spruce, European larch and white fir did not re-establish themselves in England at this time, although they had been present in pre-glacial times (Landolt *Our Alpine Flora*). The reason appears to be that during the last glaciation these species sought refuge in the central European Alps, and west of the Urals. They were, therefore, a very long way from Britain, and their return was blocked by a mass of lowland broad-leaved woods. White fir did reach Normandy, larch remaining in the Alps, and Norway spruce only reaching the Atlantic coast of Norway in Viking times.

Fleming (1988;94) and Smith (1992;168), conclude that at the end of the Stone Age, Dartmoor would have been covered with trees, except for the most exposed hilltops, which would have been species-rich heathland. Much of the forest was then dominated by oak, and in the wetter places by alder and willow, with rowan, hazel and birch. It would have been this kind of woodland the Bronze Age men, and their successors, cleared to create pasture and develop arable land for their crops.

As Edlin (1966; 89), comments, no less than eight streams of humanity came into Britain and left their mark on the forest cover in the space of three thousand, five hundred years, from 2500 BC to 1066 AD – the men of the Neolithic or New Stone Age, the Bronze Age, the Iron Age, the Romans, the Anglo-Saxons, the Danes, the Norsemen and the Normans.

It was the Bronze Age and Iron Age axes, together with the grazing of animals, that eliminated the forest cover. Hameldown was denuded of forests, and by the end of the Bronze Age, Widecombe valley was an open landscape of fields and farms – very much as we see it today (Fleming, 1988;49).

Heathercombe, because of the known habitation in the hut circles, was undoubtedly the same, leaving some oak and scrub by way of protection, and alder and willow in the lower part of the valley.

One could speculate that there was very little change in the trees in the Heathercombe valley up to about the sixth or seventh century AD, unless during this period there was an abandonment of farming, either pastural or arable, because of the deterioration of climate. There would then have been a temporary advance of trees and scrub, only to be cleared again when the climate improved during the sixth and seventh centuries AD.

As the Heathercombe valley appears to have been farmed continuously since the seventh or eighth century AD, the land would have remained clear of trees and scrub, except for protection on the steeper ground, on rocky ground and on land disturbed by tin streaming. This would have been the situation when John Kitson bought the Heathercombe valley in 1868, by which time most, but not all, of the land was pasture. The dominant species would have been pedunculate oak (*Quercus robur*), willow, hazel, beech, birch, wychelm, hawthorn and rowan (Appendix 1).

During the period 1870 to 1900, John Kitson made great improvements to the amenity of the Heatree estate, and no doubt towards the latter part of that period, in the Heathercombe valley, planted along the lower part of the valley a mixture of horse chestnut, sweet chestnut, lime, scots pine, Douglas and grand fir. He also planted substantial areas of Norway spruce, Douglas fir and European larch as forestry plantations (See Appendix 2). It was for these latter plantations that the Devon and Courtenay Clay Company purchased the Heathercombe estate in 1947, securing timber for mining purposes. The fifty to sixty year old Douglas fir was regarded as being particularly fine timber. The larch was purchased for its special suitability as mining timber in that, unlike many of the other types of timber, it resisted snapping under pressure because of its long fibre. It was therefore safe to be used as overhead timber in mines.

To enable the Devon and Courtenay Clay Company to extract this timber, it had to dedicate the estate for forestry. The dedication plan provided for a substantial amount of larch, Douglas fir and Norway spruce to be planted.

When Claude Pike purchased the estate in 1965, the planting programme had not been completed, and he introduced – particularly on the newtake – Sitka spruce. He also planted noble fir, grand fir, western hemlock and western red cedar as commercial forestry crops, whilst preserving the mixture of trees planted by John Kitson alongside the streams by way of amenity (see Appendix 3).

Claude Pike also started the development of an arboretum with the object of planting as wide a range of deciduous and coniferous trees as the height and climate would permit (schedules of trees on the estate, and those forming the arboretum, are annexed).

Tree Planting Maps 17–20		
Map 1	Pre-Kitson 1868–Mixed Hardwoods	
Map 2	Planting by John Kitson 1868–1911– Hatched area shown on 1908 Ordnance Survey as Mixed Conifer and Hardwood planting. Area coloured–Introduction of mixed Hardwoods: Lime, Sweet Chestnut, Horse Chestnut, Douglas Fir and Scots Pine.	
Map 3	Area hatched–All replanted Conifer under the Devon and Courtenay Deed of Dedication, completed by Claude Pike. Area coloured–Unchanged, although some of the Douglas have been extracted, other Hardwoods remaining.	
Map 4	Area coloured–'Nature reserve and arboretum. The remainder of the estate commercial forestry, managed on a conservation basis.	

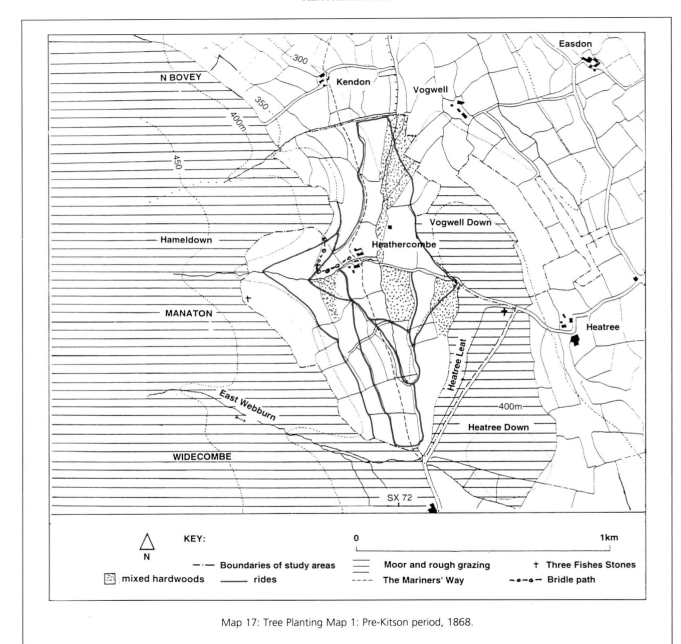

Map 17: Tree Planting Map 1: Pre-Kitson period, 1868.

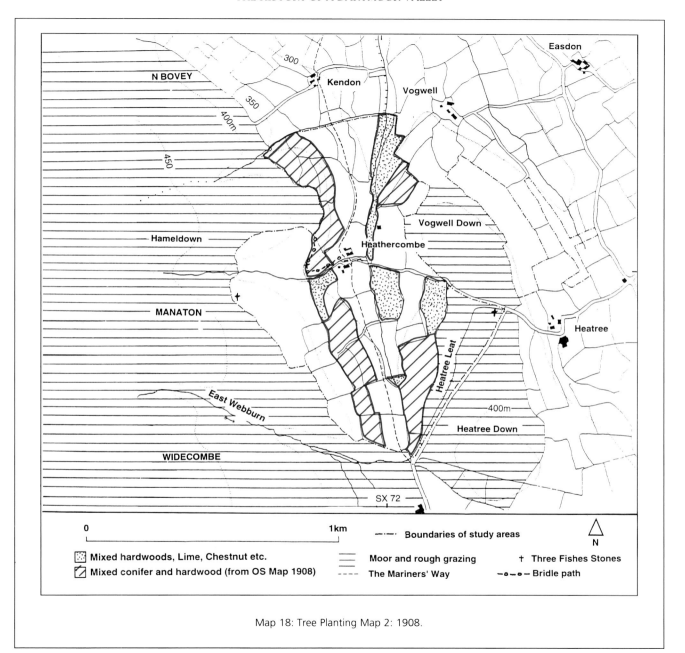

Map 18: Tree Planting Map 2: 1908.

N BOVEY

Kendon

Vogwell

Easdon

Vogwell Down

Heathercombe

Hameldown

MANATON

East Webburn

WIDECOMBE

Heatree Leat

Heatree

Heatree Down

400m

SX 72

0   1km

Boundaries of study areas

N

Mixed hardwoods, Lime, Chestnut etc.

Mixed conifer and hardwood (from OS Map 1908)

Moor and rough grazing

The Mariners' Way

Three Fishes Stones

Bridle path

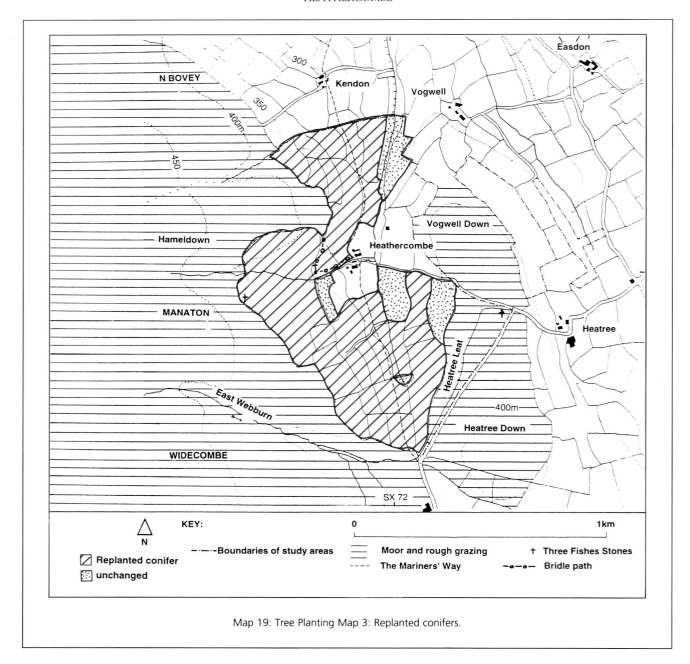

Map 19: Tree Planting Map 3: Replanted conifers.

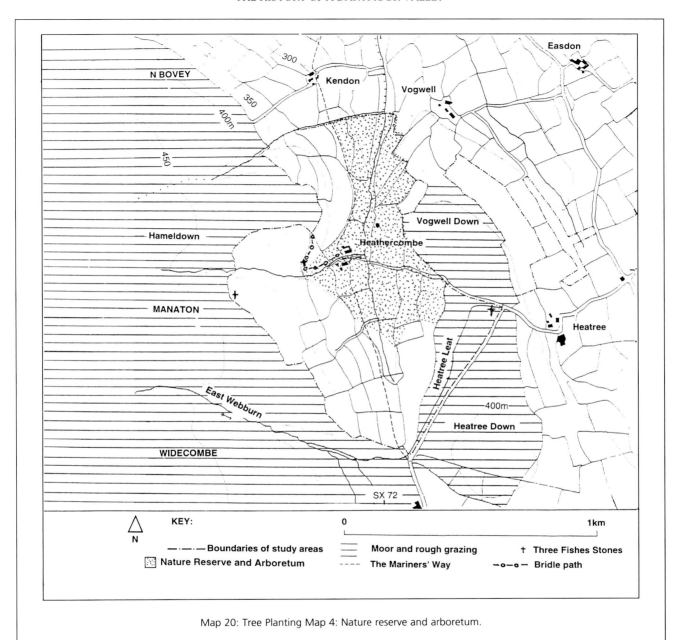

N BOVEY

300

350

400m

450

Kendon

Vogwell

Easdon

Vogwell Down

Hameldown

Heathercombe

MANATON

Heatree Leat

Heatree

WIDECOMBE

East Webburn

400m

Heatree Down

SX 72

KEY:

N

0   1km

— · — · — Boundaries of study areas

☒ Nature Reserve and Arboretum

——— Moor and rough grazing

- - - The Mariners' Way

✝ Three Fishes Stones

—o—o— Bridle path

Map 20: Tree Planting Map 4: Nature reserve and arboretum.

Appendix 1
Trees Indigenous to Heathercombe

Alder *Alnus glutinosa*
Ash *Fraxinus excelsior*
Beech *Fagus sylvatica*
Birch *Betula pendula*
Hawthorne *Cretaegus monogyna*
Hazel *Corylus avelliana*

Oak *Quercus robur*
Rowan *Sorbus aucuparia*
Sycamore *Acer pseudoplatanus*
Willow *Salix alba*
Wych Elm *Ulmus glabra*

Appendix 2
Tree Planting by John Kitson

Amenity
Giant Fir *Abies grandis*
Horse Chestnut *Aesculus hippocastanum*
Lime *Tilia platyphyllos*
Scots Pine *Pinus sylvestris*
Sweet Chestnut *Castanea sativa*
Western Red Cedar *Thuja plicata*

Forestry
Douglas Fir *Pseudotsuga menziesii*
Larch European *Larix decidua*
Norway Spruce *Picea abies*

Appendix 3
Trees Planted under Forestry Deed of Dedication by Devon and Courtenay Clay Co. Ltd.and Claude Pike

Douglas Fir *Pseudotsuga menzieii*
Giant Fir *Abies grandis*
Japanese Larch *Larix kaempferi*
Noble Fir *Abies procera*
Norway Spruce *Picea abies*
Western Red Cedar *Thuja plicata*
Western Hemlock *Tsuga heterophylla*

Appendix 4
Heathercombe Arboretum

Hardwoods

Acer – **Maple**
    capillipes
    cappadocicum
    ginnala
    griseum–Paperbark Maple
    hersii
    macrophyllum–Oregon Maple
    palmatum–Japanese Maple
        atropurpureum
        dissectum
        heptalobum
    platanoides–Norway Maple
    rubrum–Red or Canadian Maple
    saccharinum–Silver Maple
     laciniatum
    saccharum–Sugar Maple
Aesculus–**Horse Chestnut–Buckeye**
    hippocastanum–Common Horse
      Chestnut
    indica–Indian Horse Chestnut
    parviflora
Alnus–*incana aurea*–**Alder**
Betula–**Birch**
    lutea
    pendula
    papyrifera
Carpinus–**Hornbeam**
    betulus
Carya ovata– Shagbark Hickory
Castania sativa– Sweet or Spanish Chestnut
    aureomarginata
Cercidiphyllum japonicum
Crataegus oxyacantha
    orientalis
Davidia involucrata–Paper Handkerchief Tree
Eucalyptus–Gum Tree
    coccifera
Eucryphia–*glutinosa*
    hilleri winton
    nymansay
Enonymus–*alatas*
    planipes
    yedoensis

Fagus– Beech
    sylvatica
        aurea pendula
        Dawyck
        heterophylla–Cutleaved Beech
        Rohanii–Purple Cutleaved Beech
        Zlatia
Fraxinus ornus– Manna Ash
Hamamelis intermedia–Witch Hazel
Juglans– **Walnut**
    nigra
    regia–Common Walnut
Liquidambar styraciflua– Sweet Gum
Liriodendron–**Tulip Tree**
    chinense
    tulipifera
Nothofagus
    antarctica
    dombeyi
    menziesii
    obliqua
    procera
    pumilo
Nyssa sylvatica
Parrotia persica
Platanus orientalis– Oriental Plane
Populus–**Poplar**
    alba   *candicans*
    balsamifera   *trichocarpa*
Prunus avium–Gean–Wild Cherry
Pterocarya fraxinifolia–Wing Nut
Pyrus salicifolia–Willow-leaved Pear
Quercus–**Oak**
    canariensis–Algerian Oak
    castaneifolia–Chestnut-leaved Oak
    cerris–Turkey Oak
    coccinea–Scarlet Oak
    frainetto–Hungarian Oak
    kelloggii–Califorian Black Oak
    macranthera–Caucasian Oak
    palustris–Pin Oak
    petraea–Sessile or Durmast Oak
    phellos–Willow Oak

Appendix 4
(continued)

Robinia pseudoacacia–**Common Acacia**
    frisia
Salix–**Willow**
    alba–White Willow
    lanata–Woolly Willow
Sorbus aucuparia–Rowan Mountain Ash
    Aspleniifolia foliosa
    Wilfred Fox
Tilia–**Lime**
    petiolaris–Weeping Silver Lime
    platyphyllos–Broad-leaved Lime
    tomentosa–Silver Lime
Zelkova
    serrata

CONIFERS

Abies–**Silver Firs**
    alba–European Silver Fir
    cephalonica–Grecian Fir
    concolor–Colorado White Fir
    delavayi forrestii
    grandis–Giant Fir
    homolepis– Nikko Fir
    koreana–Korean Fir
    nordmanniana–Caucasian Fir
    pinsapo–Spanish Fir
    procera–Noble Fir
    veitchii
Aranucaria–*aruncara*–Chile Pine–
        Monkey Puzzle
Calocedrus–*decurrens*–Incense Cedar
Cedrus–*atlantica*–Atlas Cedar
deodara–Indian Cedar
libani–Cedar of Lebanon
Chamaecyparis–**False Cypress**
    lawsoniana   *interex*
    aureovariegata   *talanei*
    columnaris   *pottenii*
    elegantissima   *stardust*
    ellwoodii   *stewartii*
    erecta viridis   *Triomuan Baskoop*
    fletcheri   Winston Churchill
    fraserii   *Wisselii*

Cryptomeria japinica–Japanese Cedar
Cunninghamia lanceolata–Chinese Fir
Cupressocyparis leylandii
Cupressus
    arizonica
    glabra
    glabra–Blue Ice
    macrocarpa–Donard Gold
    Sempervirens stricta
Gingko biloba–**Maidenhair Tree**
Juniperas
    communis repanda
    squamata mever
    virginiana–Pencil Cedar
Metasequoia
    glyptostroboides–Dawn Redwood
Picea
    brewerana
    engelmannii
    likiangensis
    omorika–Serbian Spruce
    orientalis–Oriental Spruce
    smithiana–West Himalyan Spruce
Pinus
    aristata
    armandii
    jeffreyi
    parviflora–Japanese White Pine
    ponderosa–Western Yellow Pine
    radiata–Montery Pine
Saxegothaea conspicua–Prince Albert's Yew
Sciadopitys verticillata–Umbrella Pine
Sequoia sempervirens–Californian Redwood
Sequoiadendron giganteum–Wellingtonia
Taxodium distichum–Swamp Cypress
Taxus baccata–English Yew
Thurja occidentalis–American Arbor vitae
Thujopis delabrata
Tsuga mertensiana
    sieboldii

HEATHERCOMBE AS A NATURE RESERVE

Whilst the higher ground of the estate above the main extraction rides is managed as commercial forestry, the lower ground (as shown on Map 20) is being developed as an arboretum, and to establish what kind of trees will prosper at over 1000ft (300m) above O.D. and with special emphasis on nature conservation. The only interference with nature is the endeavour to control the grey squirrel, which does so much damage to semi-mature trees. The fox is relied upon to control the rabbits, the population of which varies from year to year.

The sides of the woodland rides are cut once a year, in the Autumn, to ensure that wild flowers are not suppressed.

The principal features of the flora and fauna are as follows:

Flora

The flowers of the valley are perhaps its most appreciated attribute from January to midsummer, before the autumn tints bring the spectacular colours of the maples, beeches, red oaks, dogwood and larch.

In January, the wild snowdrops flower profusely until early March, when they are followed by the wild daffodils which appear in different parts of the valley, especially in Fairy Wood, round Manwood house, and away over in Badger Wood.

From March to May, the yellow primrose grows on the banks in profusion, enjoying the open sunlight.

Between April and early June, bluebells appear throughout the woods on land which has never been cultivated, or not for many years. The extensive areas of bluebells are a special feature of the valley, carpeting many acres and, in part, blooming in association with the purple purslane.

During this time, the more recently planted rhododendrons and azaleas are in flower after the last frosts, until the middle of July, followed closely by the earlier planted rhododendrons–*Ponticum* and *Catawbiense*–no doubt planted by John Kitson before the turn of the century along the old woodland paths.

Soon after midsummer, particularly in the recently cleared woodland, the foxgloves, balsam and rosebay willow herb appear in profusion.

Of the less conspicuous wild flowers, the most interesting are the yellow American lily, flag iris, purple orchid, anemones, celandine, violets, euphorbia, buttercups and kingcups, with a variety of mosses and ferns in the damp, shady places.

The wild fruits of the valley are the blackberry, sloe and wild plum, with the nuts on the Hazel trees.

The moorland ling and bell heather, as well as the bilberry, have encroached in places from the neighbouring moor.

Fungi

In the autumn and early winter, fungi of all sorts erupt from the ground and trunks of the trees, alive or dead. The most unwelcome is the honey fungus (33) because of its deadly effect on nearby trees, although apparently it is edible when cooked. Otherwise, the most conspicuous and attractive is the scarlet, white-spotted fly agaric (15)–straight from a child's picture book. Although many of the fungi are deadly poisonous, the following are edible:

Chantrelles (191), amethyst deceiver (52) orange birch bolete (211), sulphur polypore (222) or 'chicken of the woods', which erupts from tree trunks, oyster (182) which grows on fallen beech timber, and apparently particularly delicious, the yellow saffron milkcap (80), which thrives on pine needles.

Fungus forays take place amongst the woods from time to time by visitors particularly interested, especially in what they can find to eat.

(Page references given to Roger Phillips *Mushrooms*, 1981).

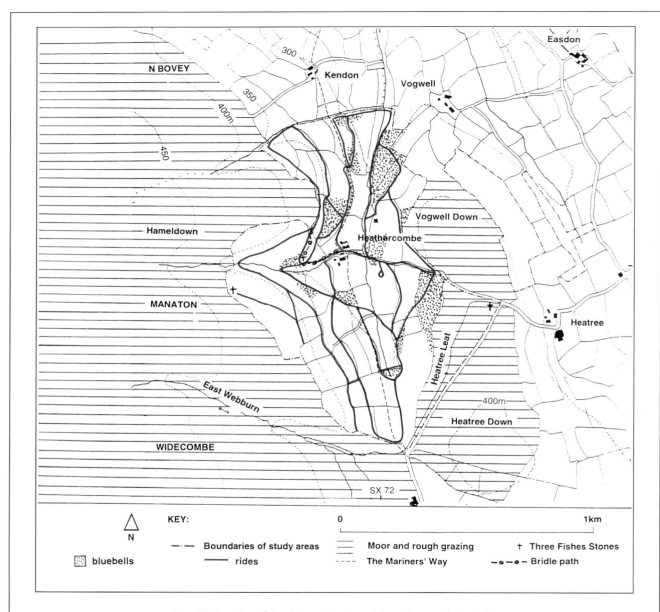

Map 21: Location of the rides within the estate and areas of bluebells.

The grounds at Heathercombe have been planted with a wide range of exotic species, chosen with regard to soil type, altitude and climate. Above (clockwise from top left) *Gunnera manicata; Sciadopitys verticillata* (umbrella pine); Bluebells (*Campanula*) carpeting the woodland floor; *Abies koreana*, the vivid purple cones of the Korean fir; *Liriodendron chinense.*

(Top right) The author and his wife at the original dwelling at Heathercombe, once a keeper's cottage. (Right) 'Manwood', built by the author to replace the original cottage. (Top left) *Populas caudicans* (Above) Spectacular autumnal colours at 'Manwood'.

(Above) Winter at North Heathercombe longhouse. (Left: clockwise from top right) A family Christmas in front of the large open fireplace at North Heathercombe; Bee boles at North Heathercombe; Fly Agaric is commonly found in the woodland in autumn (John Clements photo); Greater spotted woodpecker whose tapping echoes through the woodland (John Clements photo).

(Below) Heathercombe Brake Fox Farm.

(Top) A fox stalks through the garden in early spring. (Far left) Canada Geese are regularly visitors to the reconstructed ponds. (Left) The Holly Blue (John Clements photo).

Ferns

In the damper areas of the woodlands, there is a variety of ferns, including the buckler (84), the soft shield fern (91), and the common polypody growing on walls, trees and rocks (105), the hart's tongue (100), the hard fern, blechnum spicant (103), and the introduced royal fern (104).

Mosses

There are many kinds of mosses, but the most extensive is the *Thuidium tamariscinum* (139) and the *Polytrichum commune* (119).

Lichen

The damp climate causes lichen to grow on the trees and shrubs, particularly *Cladonia portentosa* (179).
(Page references given to Roger Phillips *Grasses, Ferns Mosses and Lichen*, 1980).

Fauna

Insects

The variation in the woodlands between shade and sunshine, from the now quite small areas of dark canopy to open ground, provides habitat for a range of insects. The profusion of wild flowers and blossom in the early summer attracts a wide range of butterflies, such as the male Brimstone (90), the tangerine-coloured male Orange Tip (90) and the Holly Blue (94).

Along the wider rides and the sunny glades, one finds the Speckled Wood (102), the Meadow Brown (106), the Silver-washed Fritillary (98), and the White Admiral (102).

(Page references from *Creating a Butterfly Garden* E.J.M. Warren, 1988).

There are even more woodland moths attracted by sallows and willows–the Puss moth, Eyed-hawk moth, and the Pebble Hook-tip, are just a few. The dead wood in the forest is an important habitat, many insect living on the rotting trunks and timbers.

The dragonflies, however, are most the attractive–the Golden-ringed dragonfly is on the wing throughout the summer and autumn. The streams. Pools and bogs are their natural habitat.

Bees have always been in profusion in the valley, as is evidenced by the six bee boles in the walls of North Heathercombe. Wasp's nests are hazards the woodmen have to take care to avoid.

Birds

When one wakes in the morning, the first birds to be seen on the balcony seeking crumbs are the robin– the most domineering, the blue tit, chaffinch and nuthatch. The heron is often seen at that time floating up the valley for its breakfast.

The thrush on the lawn, the crow in the distance, the blackbird and the increasing number of magpies are seen further afield. One sees the grey wagtail near water and ponds catching the insects on the wing. The jay is seen flying around and the buzzard gliding in the warm draughts of air on its broad wings.

In the damper part of the wood, one frequently disturbs a woodcock rising silently with its twisting flight. The sound of drumming on a dead branch betrays the greater-spotted woodpecker. In the springtime, the cuckoo is all too anxious to make its presence known.

As night falls, the tawny owl's hooting announces that its night-time hunting of mice and other small mammals has begun.

The lake at the bottom of the estate attracts Canada geese and duck as they move around from pond to pond, endeavouring to keep clear of the fox.

The only game bird in the valley is the pheasant.

Mammals

The woodlands are home to numerous mammals; their presence is largely indicated by the signs they leave. The rabbits are, of course, most conspicuous, then the fox announced by the scent it leaves behind.

Whereas the foxes tend to keep the rabbits in

check, there is, unfortunately, no natural eliminator of the grey squirrel, which does enormous damage to the trees between April and July each year by stripping bark from the ten-twenty year old hardwoods, particularly sycamore and maple, and also, frequently, beech and oak. Artificial means of control are therefore essential.

Badgers are rarely seen, but their presence is all too obvious, especially in the spring of the year when they root up the grass in search of food. Their paths are well marked between sets and their drinking places, and being clean animals, unlike the fox, the sites they select for their latrines. The presence of deer is clearly indicated by their droppings and their two-toed footprints. The roe deer are the most numerous, but red deer are beginning to frequent the woods. The rubbing of the bark of young trees, and the eating of leaders of the young saplings is an unwelcome indication of their presence, and the cause of one having to erect unsightly but appropriately tall tree guards.

Of the smaller mammals, voles and mice are ever active—by night under the watchful eye of the tawny own, and by day, the buzzard.

There are mink along the Heathercombe Brook and the side of the lake, although they are rarely seen. They eliminated the ducks we tried to establish on the lake, in spite of an island sanctuary in the lake.

Amphibians and Reptiles

Lizards are by far the commonest reptile found in the valley. Other reptiles can be found in the grassy, wetter parts of the forest, including slow-worm, grasssnake and adder. Frogs are common around the pools.

Fish

There are usually plenty of trout in the Heathercombe Brook, the ponds and the lake; as a result the heron is a regular visitor.

EARLY LAND OWNERSHIPS– GLEANINGS

At the time of the Domesday Survey (*Devon Domesday* Part 1 p.160) Edwy held Manaton from Baldwin, who held Manaton from the King, with many other parts of Devon of which he was Sheriff (*Devon Domesday* Part 2, Ch.16).

This Baldwin was the second son of Count Gilbert of Brionne, and the younger brother of Richard. They came over, invading Britain with Duke William in 1066, from Normandy. As a result, Richard was rewarded by being made Lord of Clare in Suffolk, with properties in East Anglia and East Midlands.

Baldwin was made Lord of Okehampton, Keeper of the Royal Castle and Sheriff of the County of Devon in which he was granted large estates (*Devon Domesday*, Part II Ch.16, Stenton, 1990; 630–632 and White, 1968; 32.). (For the administration of the Shire see Costen 1992; 162).

In the next reign, William II granted the barony of Okehampton to Richard de Redvers, and was created Earl of Devon by Henry I. The title later passed through Baldwin, the eighth Earl. Hugh Courtenay was descended from the sister of Baldwin de Redvers, and was created Earl of Devon in 1485. One of his successors, Henry, after being attainted, was beheaded in 1539 and his honours forfeited. The title was restored in 1553 to his son Edward, but he died in 1556 without issue and the earldom became extinct.

In 1603, Charles Blount, the eighth Baron Mountjoy, an ancestor of Miss Diana Blount now of South Heathercombe, was created Earl of Devon, but died without issue, and the title again became extinct. It was revived in 1831 when the title was restored to William Courtenay, he having established his claim to the earldom as heir to Edward who had died without issue in 1556 (White 1850;33).

The Rev. H. Fulford William MA, BD (1962), records that Little Manaton Manor was owned by

Philip de Wrexford. His son granted it to Thomas Langdon in 1232. Langdon's descendants sold the Manor to Dr Dymock, a mine magnate, in the reign of Edward IV (1442, r.1461 to 1483). This was probably the height of the tin mining in the area.

Lord Courtenay bought the Manor in about 1800. It seems clear that the Courtenay family–the Earls of Devon–who, for hundreds of years, had been large landowners in Devon–were in fact the owners of land in North Bovey, Bovey Tracey, Moreton-hampstead and Manaton (White, 1850, p.468, 469, 476 and 477) farms having been sold from time to time over the past two hundred years (White, 1968; 32–33).

The Petheridge Family

There are records that early in the eighteenth century, John Petheridge was a tenant of two tenements at Challacombe from the Earl of Devon, and that in 1840, South Middle Challacombe was leased by William Petheridge from the Earl of Devon A William Petheridge, a farmer, owned his farm in Manaton in 1850.

In the 1840s Survey, Heathercombe was included in the Manaton Parish Survey. The estate (then spelt Hethercombe) was owned and occupied by one, John Petheridge, age thirty, paying £3.5s per annum tithe to the Rector of Widecombe, and £3.10s. for the tithes of corn and grain to the Dean and Chapter of Salisbury. John Petheridge and his brother, Edward, also thirty, and sister, Charlotte, twenty-five, all lived at Heathercombe, and one, Thomas Petheridge owned and farmed Vogwell.

In 1851, Charlotte and also her sister, Betsy, lived at South Heathercombe (the Hamlyns farmed North Heathercombe).

In 1857, James Pike, farmer, lived at Heathercombe.

In 1868, a Samuel Wreford, farmer, was at Heathercombe.

James Wilcocks farmed Heathercombe in 1873 (*Devon Post Office Directory* 1873 p.237).

It was from Thomas Petheridge that the Kitsons bought Vogwell Farm on 24 December, 1872. He was

then living at Bosomzeale, Dittisham–Yeoman.

It is interesting to note that Mrs Pethybridge of Hartyland, Postbridge, was a great benefactor of St Gabriel's Church, Postbridge, having beautified the church between the wars in memory of her two brothers killed, and in memory of her family. This is a church the author and his family frequently attend.

South Heathercombe was occupied by the Kernicks in the 1880s onwards. Mr Kernick being engaged in stone wall building on the Kitson estate. Mr Kernick was Miss Hannaford's (of Widecombe) grandfather. Her mother was born at South Heathercombe.

The Nosworthy Family

The Duchy Challacombe Survey of 1991 records that in 1787, a Mr Nosworthy owned East Challacombe, he being a major landowner.

In 1850, there were Nosworthy's in Manaton–William, John and Robert.

The Kitsons bought Jay's Grave from Robert and Edith Nosworthy on 25 May, 1893.

Heathercombe Brake–The fox farm and North Heathercombe

A wooden bungalow known at Heathercombe Brake was built in the 1920s. The first tenants were Messrs Whitehead and Tindale, who started a silver fox farm. Silver fox furs were popular at the time; one, in fact, was supplied to the elegant Princess Marina, Duchess of Kent. Messrs Whitehead and Tindale were followed by a Mr Chaffey, who specialised in blue foxes until the farm was closed in the early part of the Second World War.

Miss Ellery Hull, sister of Field Marshal Sir Richard Hull KG, GCB, DSO, was at that time married to Commander Gibbons and they lived at North Heathercombe. They were divorced, leaving Mrs Gibbons living at North Heathercombe, and undertaking secretarial work at Heatree House for the Rev. John Kitson. There she met his son, Alec Kitson, and in about 1946 they were married and went to live at Heathercombe Brake. Mrs Kitson did not like living at Heathercombe Brake and moved to South Heathercombe.

In the meantime, a Captain Evans, who had been renting Burn Cottage (now Manwood) had moved to North Heathercombe. He had three boys and it was at this time that the Kitson's estate put a floor in over the old dairy at the west end of North Heathercombe, thereby creating an additional bedroom, the ground floor partition being removed to create a larger room, as it is today.

After the death of the Rev. John Kitson of Heatree, his executors distributed his estate in different ways. On 31 July, 1948, Ellery Kitson bought South Heathercombe and Burn Cottage for £2975. On the same day, Alec Kitson took over North Heathercombe which had been bequeathed to him. It was after this time that Alec and Ellery Kitson moved from South Heathercombe to North Heathercombe, where they both lived until their death.

The Rev. John Kitson's executors sold Heathercombe Brake to Miss K.K. Calton and Mrs E.M. Sheppard on 2 February, 1948, for £3625, to be used as a nursing home. This did not last long and was for sale in 1950, when Miss Quantick was first interested in it, but at that time she could not afford to buy it. The property then passed to Mr and Mrs Gaywood, and then to Mrs. Allchin. It came up for sale again in 1955, and at this time Miss Quantick was able to buy it. In 1958, Miss Quantick transferred Heathercombe Brake to the Heathercombe Brake Trust, an educational charity established to provide accommodation for deprived children sent to her, in the main, by local authorities. This became an adjunct of Heatree House which expanded enormously during the next thirty years, before going into decline in the late 1980s, the local authorities ceasing to fund the sending of children into residential care.

In 1990, Heathercombe Brake changed its activities and became a place for weekend and other activities for young people from different organisations.

During the thirty years from 1955 two additional two-storey houses were built as part of the Heathercombe Brake complex. The original wooden house was burnt down in about 1980.

THE IMPACT OF VICTORIAN PROSPERITY

We have seen how the prosperity in Queen Elizabeth I's reign (1533 r.1558–1603) and after the Restoration (1660) had its effect on the evolution of the Heathercombe longhouse. Prosperity during Queen Victoria's reign had an even greater impact on the Heathercombe and neighbouring farms, thanks to the enterprise of James Bryant, the Kitson's of Torquay and the partners of Watts, Blake, Bearne.

James Bryant—the enterprising Plymouth businessman

The brothers James and William Bryant played a leading role in the development of industry in Plymouth. They were both Quakers (Gill, 1993; 213).

In 1836, William Bryant started making starch and refining sugar with his partner, Edward James. They also factored lucifer matches.

William, with another partner, May, began to make their own matches, starting the famous firm of Bryant & May of 'Swan Vestas' fame. William Bryant's brother, James, apart from being involved in the refining of sugar, in 1844, began the manufacture of soap, which business they sold to the British and Irish sugar refining company in 1856.

The significance, as far as Heathercombe is concerned, is that James Bryant clearly invested the proceeds of this prosperity in buying farms in and around Heatree and Heathercombe, including Hedge Barton.

The Kitsons of Torquay

James Bryant sold the Heatree and Heathercombe farms to John and Robert Kitson in 1863, and a little later, Hedge Barton farm to John's cousin, Walter Kitson, they being able to buy and develop these farms thanks to the wealth acquired in the development of Torquay in the first half of the nineteenth century (see the following section).

Watts, Blake, Bearne—the development of the South Devon Ball Clay Industry

The prosperity of the Victorian era enabled the partnership of Watts, Blake, Bearne, founded in 1861, to develop as one of the leading suppliers of plastic clay to the ceramic industry. This partnership prospered and expanded into the twentieth century, Claude Pike joining the company in 1945. It was the result of the continued success of this company that Claude Pike was able to acquire the Heathercombe estate (see the chapter–Claude Pike–Heathercombe as an Amenity Estate).

THE KITSONS AT HEATHERCOMBE 1868–1947

THE LEISURE PURSUIT OF A TORQUAY LAWYER AND BANKER

John and Robert Kitson were the sons of William Kitson 'the Maker of Torquay', born 6 April, 1800. William was 'a great and good man, and did great and good work'.

William Kitson was steward of the property of the Palk family, who owned, and in the first half of the nineteenth century, developed a substantial part of Torquay, mostly to the east of Fleet Street, on land purchased by Sir Robert Palk in 1768. His wealth was gained as Governor of Madras, and inherited from Stringer Lawrence, building Haldon Belvedere in his memory. The Palk family thereafter included Lawrence as one of their Christian names.

William Kitson was also the lawyer and banker for the Cary family who owned Torre Abbey and surrounding land. William Kitson was educated at Blundell's School and became a solicitor, entering into practice in Torquay in 1826—then little more than a hamlet in the parish of Torre. In 1831, with a Mr Vivian, he started a Torquay bank—Vivian, Kitson & Co., taken over by Lloyds Bank in 1908.

John Kitson was born in 1835. Educated at Marlborough College, he qualified as a lawyer and joined the law firm, W. and C. Kitson, and in 1863, became a partner in the Torquay bank, Vivian, Kitson & Co. He was given the Freedom of Torquay in 1909.

Robert Kitson was born in 1843, and was educated at Marlborough and Balliol College, Oxford. He became a partner in the Torquay bank, but died at Cannes in 1885.

North and South Heathercombe, along with North and South Heatree farms, were purchased by John and Robert Kitson on 1 January, 1868 from James Bryant of Plymouth. Vogwell, including Title 349 'Mill Pits', was purchased from Thomas Pethybridge on 24 December, 1872.

On 1 January, 1885, John Kitson bought from his brother, Robert, his half-share in Heatree, North Heathercombe and South Vogwell, Kendon and North Easdon.

On 25 May, 1893, he bought Jay's Grave from Robert and Elizabeth Nosworthy.

John Kitson built Heatree House. Although the Abstract of Title of the Heathercombe property shows that John and Robert Kitson bought the Heathercombe and Heatree Farms on 1 January, 1868, the Kitsons' records state that in 1866, their father, William Kitson 'bought a large tract of partly cultivated moorland in the Parish of Manaton on which he built a house called Heatree, and this he constantly visited, and also entertained many friends who much enjoyed the beautiful air and scenery of Dartmoor.' This seems to be confirmed, for in the Post Office Guide of 1873, amongst the four most important landowners was William Kitson (He died in 1883.). Another was the Earl of Devon.

Morris's *Directory for Devon* 1870 records John and Robert Kitson, and William Kitson all living at Heatree, and James Bryant at Hedge Barton. This must be the same James Bryant of Hedge Barton who is reported to have excavated Jay's Grave in about 1860. Hedge Barton was acquired by John Kitson's cousin, Walter Kinlock Kitson.

Dymond (1876) in his *Widecombe-in-the-Moor*, mentioned a strongly built dwelling at Heatree.

White's Directory (1878) just refers to John Kitson at Heatree House. John Kitson, at a later date, was Churchwarden at Manaton.

E. Hemery, in *High Dartmoor* in 1983, records that Heatree House was the original of Baskerville Hall in Conan Doyle's *The Hound of the Baskervilles*.

Having consolidated the Heatree estate, John Kitson made great improvements, building waterfalls, ponds and lakes on the streams, erecting new stone walls and planting a wide variety of trees, particularly in the bottom part of the Heathercombe valley—lime, horse chestnut, sweet chestnut, Scots pine, Douglas fir, Lawson cyprus, beech and oak, plus plantations of Norway spruce, larch and Douglas fir (See Appendices 2 and 4).

Miss Deborah Hannaford of Widecombe, records that her grandfather worked for Mr Kitson, and helped to build the new walls towards the end of the nineteenth century, and wonders how much of the reaves were taken for this purpose, particularly on the west side of Heatree Down.

John Kitson died in 1911, leaving the Heatree estate to his godson and first cousin, John Archibald Kitson, Clerk in Holy Orders.

John Archibald Kitson died on 22 January, 1947 at Heatree, the amenity of Heathercombe having been neglected.

The Road into the Valley

The former road or tract into the valley came up from what is now called Long Lane and Kendon.

This was the parish road, but when the Kitsons acquired all the land in the district this was closed as a parish road. The main road into the valley then became the one down the steep hill direct from Heatree Down.

There was probably no vehicular traffic into the valley until the late eighteenth or early nineteenth century, the pack horse being the means of transport (Torr, 1979, Vol II 1 & 5, Hoskins, 1953–150, and Hayter Hames, 1981–85)

Dymond in his *Widecombe-in-the-Moor* writes: 'in 1876 there were packhorses only until lately. Dartmoor is no place for travellers of weak nerves or carriages with feeble springs'.

CLAUDE PIKE–HEATHERCOMBE AS AN AMENITY ESTATE 1965–1991

THE LEISURE PURSUIT OF A LAWYER AND INDUSTRIALIST

On 9 February, 1948, the Devon and Courtenay Clay Company Limited purchased plantations and moorland containing 212.431 acres at Heatree and Heathercombe from the Executors of John Archibald Kitson for £12 500.

The Devon and Courtenay Clay Company purchased the property for its timber, particularly for mining purposes. To enable it to extract the timber, it entered into a Deed of Dedication dated 15 April 1952 with the Forestry Commission, dedicating the whole estate for forestry. In consequence, when it had extracted all the timber it required, it had to carry out a phased plan of replanting the estate, particularly with Conifers, in accordance with the Deed of Dedication. The estate clearly had been neglected since the death of John Kitson in 1911.

The Devon and Courtenay Clay Company Limited was taken over by Watts, Blake, Bearne & Company Limited, of which Claude Pike was Chairman and Managing Director, in 1964. The assets of the company included the Heathercombe estate. This had no immediate value to Watts, Blake, Bearne & Company Limited; on the contrary, it carried with it the obligation to replant over the next twenty years or more. It was therefore put up for sale by Jacksons, Stopps & Staff. Claude Pike, being interested in forestry, purchased the estate in 1955 for £10 650 at Jackson, Stopps & Staff's valuation, and accepted the obligation to complete the development plan previously agreed with the Forestry Commission. This replanting was completed during the following years.

The purchase by the Devon and Courtenay Clay Company Limited did not include North Heathercombe and South Heathercombe, the adjoining paddocks and Burn Cottage (subsequently called Manwood).

South Heathercombe and Burn Cottage (Manwood)

On 31 July, 1948, Frances Ellery Kitson of Heathercombe, Manaton, wife of Alexander Frederick Kitson (and sister of Field-Marshal Sir Richard Hull, KG, GCB, DSO) purchased from the Executors of J.A. Kitson South Heathercombe and Burn Cottage for £2975. Ellery Kitson sold South Heathercombe, on 3 June, 1960, to John and Joan Turner. In 1965 Mr Rushton of Fountain Forestry was tenant.

Mr and Mrs Chapman owned South Heathercombe between 1966 and 1979 when Mr Chapman died, and Mrs Chapman sold South Heathercombe to Miss Diana Blount, sister of Sir Walter Edward Alpin Blount, twelfth Baronet (1642).

On 11 October, 1965, Ellery Kitson sold Burn Cottage, its drive and the stables, and small paddock adjoining South Heathercombe, also the road alongside North Heathercombe, to Claude Pike for £1000.

Claude Pike rebuilt the condemned Burn Cottage in 1966–1967 and renamed it Manwood, after the first lawyer to write, in 1598, a treatise on forest laws, which he had studied in preparation for writing a thesis for Cambridge University Doctorate of Law on the subject of trees.

The cottage had been built in the 1890s as a game keeper's two-bedroomed bungalow, the only water supply being taken from a well in the garden, delivering water to a drainpipe outside the back door. There was no internal plumbing or septic tank. Water had to be brought into the house by a bucket, although clothes washing took place in an outside wash-house.

The building was in such poor condition that practically the whole of it had to be taken down.

When the cottage was rebuilt to Mr Pike's design, based on an Italian mountain chalet, the architect was Arthur Newcombe, and the builders were Staverton Builders, a subsidiary of Dartington Hall.

North Heathercombe

John Archibald Kitson, who died on 22 January, 1947, in his will left North Heathercombe to his son, Alexander Frederick Kitson. This was conveyed to Alexander Frederick Kitson on 31 July, 1948.

On 11 August, 1966 Alexander Frederick Kitson died.

On 20 February, 1967, Claude Pike purchased North Heathercombe from the personal representatives of Alexander Frederick Kitson for £6100. The following year, he modernised it with up-to-date services, whilst retaining its features as a longhouse.

On 5 November, 1985, Claude Pike gave North Heathercombe to his son and daughter, John Drew Pike and Penelope Anne Drew Holland.

Heatree Down

On 31 July, 1987, Claude Pike bought Heatree Down

(21 acres–unfenced) from Mrs N.J. Bradford for £300.

Twenty-five Years (1966–1991)

In the twenty-five years following 1966, while completing the afforestation of the Heathercombe estate, as required by the Forestry Commission, Claude Pike constructed numerous new access rides, and restored the perimeter fences. He developed the lower part of the estate as an amenity for nature conservation, and by planting a wide variety of trees and shrubs, he established an arboretum of trees of the type which grow at an altitude of 1000–1100 feet (the forestry estate reaches 1400 feet). (See Appendices 3–4).

The ponds and the lake, found full and overgrown, were emptied, repaired and reinstated, and numerous paths and bridges constructed throughout the amenity area.

DARTMOOR NATIONAL PARK

There was pressure before the Second World War in favour of Dartmoor becoming a national park. In 1937, the Dartmoor Preservation Association passed the following Resolution:

'That the Association re-affirmed its express belief that the best interests of the nation, and of all having rights in or over Dartmoor, would be most readily and fully secured by the creation of a National Park to include the Forest of Dartmoor and the Commons of Devon.'

After the war, the pressure continued, culminating in the Dower Report of 1945. This report was considered and the conclusions published in 1947. Two-and-a-half years later, the National Parks and Access to the Countryside Act received royal assent, and Dartmoor's designation as a National Park was confirmed on 30 October, 1951. (The map on page 4 shows the present boundary of the Dartmoor National Park).

HEATHERCOMBE CROSSES

DOXOLOGY TO THE LORD'S PRAYER– MAN'S ULTIMATE RESPONSIBILITY

The Fishes Stones

These were erected by Claude Pike. They are rough granite posts, each about 5 feet tall. On each post a panel has been cut, and inside the panel are three fishes in relief. This was an early symbol of the Christian religion, the letters of the Greek word for fish being the first letters of the phrase 'Jesus Christ, Son of God, Saviour.' In addition, each stone bears an incised inscription of the doxology of the Lord's Prayer.

The first stone, erected in 1969, stands at the junction of the Natsworthy valley road and the lane that leads to Heathercombe, and has the inscription 'Thine is the Power'. The second stone, erected at Easter in 1971, stands on the right of the steep and winding lane that leads to Heathercombe Brake, and has the inscription 'and the Kingdom'. The third stone, erected in 1977, stands just inside the moor gate to Heathercombe Newtake, at an altitude of about 1400 feet. This has the inscription 'and the Glory'.

These stones record the owner's philosophy of man's stewardship; power derived from whatever source, to be exercised responsibly as a steward. Similarly, the Kingdom—all one's worldly assets to be held on trust; and finally, the beneficial outcome to be for the Glory of the Lord.

F.A. Starkey says: 'The result has been the erection of three beautiful and dignified artefacts to add to the splendours of the Dartmoor landscape.' (Starkey, 1984; 12 and 18. Hayward, 1991; 154).

BIBLIOGRAPHY

BARING-GOULD S. *A Book of Devon,* Methuen & Co., 1925.

BRADLEY, I. *The Celtic Way,* Darton Longman Todd, 1993.

BUTLER J. *Dartmoor Atlas of Antiquities Volume 1, The East,* Devon Books 1991.

CHANDLER M.E.J. *The Ogliocene Flora of the Bovey Basin,* 1957.

CLAYDEN A.W. *The History of Devon Scenery,* Chatto and Windus, 1906.

COSTEN M. *The Origins of Somerset,* Manchester University Press 1992.

CROSSING W. *Dartmoor Worker,* David & Charles, 1966.

CROSSING W. *Guide to Dartmoor,* David & Charles, 1965.

DEVON ARCHAEOLOGICAL SOCIETY *Prehistoric Dartmoor in its Context,* No. 37, 1979.

DURRANCE AND LAMING *Geology of Devon,* Exeter University Press, 1992.

DYER *Ancient Britain,* Batsford, 1990.

DYMOND, R. *Widecombe-in-the-Moor,* 1876.

EDLIN H.L. *Trees, Woods and Man,* Collins, 1966.

ELLIS P.B. *Celt and Saxon,* Constable, 1993.

ELWES H.J. and HENRY A.H. *The Trees of Great Britain* R & R Clark, 1913

FINBERG H.P.R. *West Country Historical Studies,* David & Charles, 1961.

FLEMING A. *The Dartmoor Reaves,* Batsford Ltd, 1988.

FULFORD WILLIAMS Rev. H. *Manaton* (n.d.)

GIBB J.H.P. *The Book of Sherborne,* Barracuda Books, 1980.

GILL C. *Dartmoor—A New Study,* David & Charles, 1970.

GILL C. *The Duchy of Cornwall,* David & Charles, 1987.

GILL C. *Plymouth—A New History,* Devon Books, 1993.

GREEVES T. *The Archaeology of Dartmoor From the Air,* Devon Books, 1985.

HARRIS H. *Industrial Archaeology of Dartmoor,* David & Charles, 1968.

HAWKES J.O.C. *Prehistoric Britain,* Pelican, 1958.

HAYTOR-HAMES J. *A History of Chagford,* Phillimore & Co., 1981.

HEMERY E. *Walking Dartmoor's Ancient Tracks,* David & Charles, 1986.

HAYWARD J. *Dartmoor 365,* Curlew Publications, 1991.

HOSKINS W.G. *Devon,* Devon Books, 1992.

JAMES N.D.G. *A History of English Forestry,* Blackwell, 1981.

MANWOOD J. *Forest Laws,* 1615.

MILDREN J. *Saints of the South-West,* Bossiney Books, 1988.

MITCHELL A. *The Gardener's Book of Trees,* Dent, 1981.

LANDOLT E. *Our Alpine Flora,* SAC Publications, Switzerland, 1989.

ORME N. *Unity and Variety—A History of the Church in Devon and Cornwall,* Exeter U.P. 1991.

PEARCE S. *The Kingdom of Dumnonia,* Lodenek Press, 1978.

PENNINGTON R.R. *Stannary Law,* David & Charles, 1973.

RACKMAN O. *The History of the Countryside,* Dent, 1987.

RISDON, STEVENS and WHITWORTH. *A Glimpse of Dartmoor,* Peninsula Press, 1992.

ROGERS J. *English Woodland,* Batsford, 1942.

ROWE S. *A Perambulation of Dartmoor,* Devon Books, 1985.

SELLMAN R.R. *Aspects of Devon History,* Devon Books, 1985.

ST. LEGER-GORDON R. *The Witchcraft and Folklore of Dartmoor,* Robert Hale, 1965.

SMITH C. *Late Stone Age Hunters of the British Isles,* Routledge, 1992.

STANES R. *The Old Farm,* Devon Books, 1990.

STARK E. *Saint Endellion,* Dyllansow Truran, 1983.

STARKEY F.H. *Dartmoor Crosses and Some Ancient Tracks,* privately published, 1983.

STARKEY F.H. *Odds and Ends from Dartmoor,* privately published, 1984.

STENTON Sir R. *Anglo-Saxon England,* Oxford University Press, 1980.

TODD M. *The South-West to AD 1000,* Longmans, 1987.

TORR C. *Small Talk at Wreyland,* Oxford University Press, 1979.

TREVELLION G.M. *History of England,* OUP, 1941

WHITE *Devon 1850,* David & Charles, 1968.

WORTH R.H. *Dartmoor,* David & Charles, 1967.

First published in Great Britain in 1993
by Westcountry Books

Copyright © 1993 Claude Pike

British Library Cataloguing in Publication Data
The CIP Record for this publication
is available from the British Library

ISBN 1-898386-02-1

WESTCOUNTRY BOOKS

Sales and publishing
1 Chinon Court, Lower Moor Way, Tiverton
Devon EX16 6SS   Tel 0884 243242 Fax 0884 243325

All photographs are from the author's collection except for the cover photos of Heathercombe Valley and longhouse (front) and Jay's Grave (back) by Stephen Woods who also supplied photos on pages 2, 11, 23, 24, 51, 52, 62, 66. Additional photos by John Clements.

Designed by Topics Visual Information, Exeter

Typeset by Exe Valley Dataset, Exeter
Printed and bound by BPCC Wheatons Ltd, Exeter